Prayers
to Share

Year B

Dedication

This book is dedicated to the church members and friends who,
through all the Sundays of the church year, have shared prayers with me.
We have offered prayers to God at

Ipswich Road United Reformed Church, Norwich, England
Lakenham United Reformed Church, Norwich, England
Princes Street United Reformed Church, Norwich, England
Knox United Church (Pruden Street), Thunder Bay, Canada
First Church United, Thunder Bay, Canada
St. Andrew's United Church, Schreiber, Canada
Terrace Bay Community Church, Terrace Bay, Canada
Westminster United Church, Thunder Bay, Canada
Duff United Church, Duff, Canada
Grace United, Lemberg, Canada
Knox United, Abernethy, Canada
St. Andrew's, Balcarres, Canada

David Sparks

PRAYERS TO SHARE YEAR B

Responsive Prayers
for each Sunday of
the Church Year

Revised Common Lectionary based

WOOD LAKE BOOKS

Editor: Mike Schwartzentruber
Cover design: Margaret Kyle
Proofreading: Dianne Greenslade

Wood Lake Books Inc. acknowledges the financial support of the Government of Canada, through
the Book Publishing Industry Development Program (BPIDP) for our publishing activities.
At Wood Lake Books we practice what we publish, guided by a concern for fairness, justice,
and equal opportunity in all of our relationships with employees and customers.
We recycle and reuse and encourage readers to do the same. Resources are printed on
recycled paper and more environmentally friendly groundwood papers (newsprint),
whenever possible. The trees used are replaced through donations to the Scoutrees for
Canada program. A percentage of all profit is donated to charitable organizations.

National Library of Canada Cataloguing in Publication Data

Sparks, David, 1938–
Prayers to share, year B
Includes index.
ISBN 1-55145-479-3

1. Common lectionary (1992). Year B.   2. Pastoral prayers.   3. Church
year – Prayer-books and devotions – English.   I. Title.
BV250.S62 2002   264'.13   C2002-910646-X

Published by
Wood Lake Books Inc.
9025 Jim Bailey Rd
Kelowna, BC V4V 1R2
www.joinhands.com

Printing 10 9 8 7 6 5 4 3 2 1

Printed in Canada by Transcontinental Printing

Contents

Because this is the first in an intended three-volume series,
the publisher and author would like to give you, the reader,
the opportunity to comment on this book and to suggest changes, additions,
or improvements that you would like to see in the upcoming volumes.
Please send your comments via e-mail to editor Mike Schwartzentruber, at
mikes@woodlake.com.

Preface

To pray, to give thanks and praise to God, who has given us everything and without whom we are nothing, is the most natural act in the world. To be able to pray with other members of the faith community Sunday by Sunday is an awesome privilege.

But what form should this public prayer take?

I believe that prayer in worship is not just a solo act of the minister, priest, or lay worship leader. Nor is it an unthinking chorus of leader and people together. It is, or should be, a dynamic, responsive act that captures the hearts and minds of congregational members and brings glory to God.

There is a solid, scriptural basis for our prayers to be found in the *Revised Common Lectionary*. Through the lectionary, the seasons of the church year are followed and the wide spectrum of the scriptures, Hebrew and Christian, is honored. Many of the prayers in this book derive from or are inspired by the readings appointed for a particular week or season.

It is my hope that those who lead worship will be helped in different ways by the weekly set of prayers provided here. Some of you will find that my style fits well with your own style, and that you can use these prayers as they are printed. Some of you will want to change words or phrases, so that you feel comfortable with them and so that the congregation can sense that the prayers are in tune with their joys, hopes, fears, and with the situation of their faith community. And, no doubt, some of you will simply want to look at the prayer patterns and work out your own themes and words for a particular week: for example, in the "Confession" prayers, I have tended not to use the traditional "miserable offender" approach but to offer affirmations, reminders, encouragement, and questions instead.

For years and years, the sermon has been considered by many to be the center of the worship experience. In my experience, it is certainly the thing most often commented on by people as they leave the worship service. I believe, however, that a worship service should be a thematic whole and that the prayers, hymns, sermon, music, and dramatic presentation should complement, reflect, and build on one another. Moreover, it is "liturgy" (the work of the people) that we are about. Worship leaders are responding faithfully when the congregation is engaged in worship and what better way of engaging the congregation than through active, responsive participation in prayers throughout the service?

As I complete this task, I am acutely aware of the ways in which the members of the pastoral charges I have served have fed my prayer life. It is their joy, their challenges, their questions, their tough places, and their reflections on scripture that are mirrored in these pages. To them, and to the One All-Loving God, I offer my profound thanks.

Advent 1

(Begins on the first Sunday of Advent in 2002, 2005, 2008, 2011…)

Isaiah 64:1–9
Psalm 80:1–7, 17–19
1 Corinthians 1:3–9
Mark 13:24–37

Call to Worship

One: A child's eyes light up as she imagines a dancing, laughing time, far, far in the future.

All: **An old person dreams of a day when infirmity and anxiety will cease.**

Choir: *A wise person reflects on the untapped potential within humanity – the potential to build a world where joy and sharing prevail.*

All: **And we, gathered in the name of Christ, catch a glimpse of Advent hope.**

Opening Prayer

One: Your presence is revealed in the light of hope, O God. The light of hope shines brightly.

All: **Joyfully we worship, for your graceful gift of Jesus is at hand.**

One: The light of hope overcomes the darkness.

All: **Joyfully we know that the powerful ones, and the terror-bringers, will not have their own way.**

One: The light of hope reveals the needs of home and community.

All: **Joyfully we will work to support the downhearted, and to show friendship to the lonely.**

One: Your presence is revealed in the light of hope, O God.

All: **The light of hope will go before us on our Advent journey.**

Prayer of Hopefulness (Confession)

One: You come to life in hope, loving God.

All: **In those times when we confront the despair that deadens us,**

One: you are alive!

All: **In those situations where we refuse to give in to the dark and self-serving powers,**

One: you are alive!

All: In the ways that cause us pain, but keep our conscience clear,

One: you are alive!

All: In the light at the end of the dark and turbulent tunnel,

One: you are alive!

All: In the will of the faith community to work with zest,

One: you are alive!

> *Time of reflection…*

Words of Assurance

One: As we experience hope, living God,

All: as new paths and fresh opportunities open up before us, we experience the peaceful energy of your presence.

One: In God's presence you are free women and men.

All: Thanks be to God! Amen.

Offering Prayer

One: We offer these gifts for your use, O God.

**All: We offer them for careful use among the suffering;
we offer them for gentle use among the hurting;
we offer them for encouraging use among the dispirited;
we offer them for use worldwide, in faith communities;
we offer them for worship, teaching, and service within this faith community;
we offer ourselves, our time and our talent, for use with our gifts.**

One: God will bless your *hopeful* offering!

All: Thanks be to our gracious God! Amen.

Commissioning

One: In the darkened sky that hangs over humanity, hope seems a futile dream.

All: But we have hope as we leave this church.

One: Hope stirs in the resolution to celebrate the joys of each day.

All: Hope stirs as we assert our confidence in the Christian community.

One: Hope comes clear when we pass through the testing times, battered but unbroken.

All: Our hope finds a focus in the journey of a young couple to Bethlehem 2000 years ago – a journey in which we join.

Advent 2

Isaiah 40:1–11
Psalm 85:1–2, 8–13
2 Peter 3:8–15a
Mark 1:1–8

Call to Worship

One: On Jordan's bank stands the prophet John.

All: John hears God's Word spoken loud and clear.

One: The prophet listens carefully to the Word and acts.

All: John's clear message brings people together to face realities.

One: The prophet recognizes the supreme worth of Jesus Christ.

All: And we, the followers of Jesus, offer worship and prayer and service, in the name of God's Anointed One.

Opening Prayer

One: Peace is your gracious gift, O God.

All: We give thanks for the Advent promise of peace, revealed in the coming of Jesus Christ.

One: Peace is your cherished gift, O God.

All: We give thanks for the opportunity to receive peace and to share peace in this faith community.

One: Peace is your challenging gift, O God.

All: We give thanks for the ways in which we can share peace, in this nation and in this neighborhood.

One: Peace is your eternal gift, O God.

All: We rejoice that, in Jesus, we have the hope of peace, which encompasses heaven and earth, time and eternity. Amen.

Prayer of Confession

One: The wilderness was the place where God's Word came to John the Baptist.

All: Give us the wisdom, O God, to take the time to listen to your word for us.

One: The wilderness was the place where the people of Israel, sorely tested, turned to worship gods of their own making.

All: Give us the strength, O God, to identify the idols that claim our allegiance and to destroy them.

One: The wilderness was the place where Jesus ventured out to prepare for his ministry and was tempted.

All: Give us, O God, the courage to face temptations and the will to be a part of an outward- and forward-looking faith community.

Time of reflection...

Words of Assurance
One: Peace is flowing like a river.
All: The peace that comes through careful reflection.
One: Peace is flowing like a river.
All: The peace of well-chosen words and action.
One: Peace is flowing like a river.
All: The peace of God, which refreshes body, mind, and spirit.
One: Receive God's peace.
All: Thanks be to God. Amen.

Offering Prayer
One: Peace is your gift, O God.
All: The peace of generosity,
the peace of compassion,
the peace of recognition,
the peace of fellowship.
One: Bless these gifts, O God, which will convey the peace of Jesus Christ. Amen.

Commissioning
One: John, by the river Jordan,
All: calls us to reflect carefully and to repent.
One: John, by the river Jordan,
All: calls us to stand beside the confused and the unfulfilled ones and to give them purpose.
One: John, by the river Jordan,
All: calls us to acknowledge the graceful influence of Jesus Christ and to renew our discipleship.

Advent 3

Isaiah 61:1–4, 8–11
Psalm 126 or Luke 1:47–55
1 Thessalonians 5:16–24
John 1:6–8, 19–28

Call to Worship

One: Joy will be felt around the world,

All: **when the oppressed receive the Good News.**

One: Joy will break out around the world,

All: **when the broken-hearted are given support.**

One: Joy will be celebrated around the world,

All: **when those held captive know freedom.**

One: Joy will be experienced around the world,

All: **when the everlasting joy of God finds expression and purpose in worship.**

Opening Prayer

One: Jesus, we will search among the most powerful nations, and not find you.

All: **Jesus, we will search among the most religious men and women, and not find you.**

One: Jesus, we will search among the momentous events of our time, and not find you.

All: **Jesus, we will search high and low, in palace, in government, and in church, and not find you.**

One: Jesus, you will surprise us.

All: **You will reveal yourself to us in an unexpected call for justice, in an unseen deed of compassion, and in a caring and empowered community.**

Prayer of Confession

One: To Mary, unsure and unprepared, came the call to serve her God.

All: **Keep us open, O God, to your call, wherever, and whenever it may come to us.**

One: To Mary, came the call to leave the tried and tested ways behind and to venture out.

All: **Keep us alert, O God, to the need to tread unfamiliar pathways, knowing you will go with us.**

One: To Mary, an ordinary young woman, came the call to accept a radical change in her life's pattern.

All: **Enable us to face, O God, the risk of faithfulness and our regrets over what has been left behind.**

One: To Mary, came a call to understand and accept God's presence in her life.

All: **Keep us sensitive, O God, to your presence in the routine of our lives, and to the faithful messengers who come unbidden to guide us.**
Time of reflection…

Words of Assurance

One: As we struggle to find and do your will, O God, we will find a model of gracious acceptance in your servant Mary. She frees us to walk your hard way with courage.

All: **In thorough reflection, and with a renewed dedication to a life that is caring, questioning, inspiring, and hopeful, will come pardon and peace. Thanks be to God! Amen.**

Offering Prayer

One: Bring us down to earth, living God.

All: **In our offering, may we accept the reality of proclaiming the Good News in word and deed today.**

One: The reality is that without gifts shared, talents used, and time made available, Christ's work cannot be done and your realm will not come closer.

All: **As you bless these gifts, O God, grant us wisdom to use them in the Way of Jesus. Amen.**

Commissioning

One: Christ is coming, rejoice!

All: **From generation to generation we are blessed.**

One: Christ is coming, rejoice!

All: **The lowly will receive confidence, the powerful will be put in their place.**

One: Christ is coming, rejoice!

All: **There is hope for the poor and the hungry.**

One: Christ is coming, rejoice!

All: **God, faithful in times past, will remain faithful to us and to our church.**

Advent 4

2 Samuel 7:1–11, 16
Luke 1:47–55 or Psalm 89:1–4, 19–26
Romans 16:25–27
Luke 1:26–38

Call to Worship
One: First-born of Mary and Joseph from Nazareth, born lowly, yet born to
be the Savior, Savior of the world:
All: **may all nations see the Savior's face, the face that loves us into
justice and sharing.**
One: Savior of the church:
All: **may we who are disciples see the Savior's face, the face that loves us
into community.**
One: Savior of the human heart:
All: **may each of us see the Savior's face, the face that loves us into
compassion.**

Opening Prayer
One: The rich food and special drinks, the cakes and candies, give us the
satisfied feelings we look for,
All: **but God's love will be cradled before us, a love which is all we need.**
One: The "bargains" in the store windows shout loudly of the gifts we
must have,
All: **but God's love will be cradled before us, a love which is all we need.**
One: The soap operas and the Christmas movies make clear the romance so
many are seeking,
All: **but God's love will be cradled before us, a love which is all we need.**
One: Wonderful God, we rejoice that Jesus, vulnerable but rooted in your
love, is coming to us this Christmas.
All: **Our thanks is heartfelt! Amen.**

A Reflective Prayer (Confession)
One: Look into Mary's face; see the reluctance, feel the anxiety. Why should
she be the one to bear this awesome child?

All: **When we are called on to pursue the unforeseen yet faithful task, how do we respond?**

One: Look into Mary's face; see the uncertainty, feel the fear. Why should she be the one to bear this child of God?

All: **When we are called on to venture out in new ways, how do we respond?**

One: Look into Mary's face; see the growing trust, feel the acceptance. Why should she not be God's servant?

All: **When we are called on to respond confidently and to work whole-heartedly, how do we respond?**

Time of silence...

Words of Assurance

One: Put the uncertainty, the lack of trust, and the lack of confidence behind you. The past no longer holds you in its grip.

All: **We are resolved to go forward as faithful servants of God.**

One: As trusted servants, God will support you and you will experience God's peace.

All: **Thanks be to God. Amen.**

Offering Prayer

One: Love shone from the stable at Bethlehem; love will come clear from these offerings:

All: **a love that reaches out to link hands with the suffering,**
a love that encourages the dispirited,
a love that will accept the vulnerable,
a love worked out in faith community,
a love that crosses oceans and ethnic groups.

One: A Jesus-type love.

All: **In his name these offerings will be blessed. Amen.**

Commissioning

One: Go with joy!

All: We are ready to welcome God's Most Precious One.

One: Go with peace!

All: We are prepared to welcome the Prince of Peace.

One: Go with hope!

All: We understand that from darkness, light will shine forth.

One: Above all, go with love!

All: We realize that God's love in Christ, is for us, and for all humankind.

Christmas Day/Eve

Proper I (A, B, C)

Isaiah 9:2–7
Psalm 96
Titus 2:11–14
Luke 2:1–14, (15–20)

Call to Worship

One: Jesus is born to change our darkness to light;
All: the light from the stable has become the Light of the World.
One: Jesus is born to change our sadness to joy;
All: the joy of the shepherds still echoes down the years.
One: Jesus is born to give hope to the oppressed;
All: God's love within a persecuted family inspires us.
One: Jesus is born!
**All: And we rejoice that on this day of all days (night of all nights),
         we can come and worship!**

Opening Prayer

One: The waiting is over; God's Anointed One is here!
All: We will praise God for the coming of Jesus Christ.
One: The journey is over; Mary's son is born!
All: We will praise God for the gift of a Savior.
One: Darkness is overcome; light blazes from the lowly stable.
All: We will praise God, for hope alive in a tiny child.
One: Conflict is overcome; there is calm over the whole earth.
All: We will praise God, for the One who brings peace.

Prayer of Confession

One: This is the wonder of Christmas: that we are united in praise and worship.
All: When we fail to give thanks and prayer and praise, O God, forgive us.
One: This is the joy of the Christmas season: that compassion flourishes and
     relationship is restored.
All: When we fail to reach out friendship's hand, O God, forgive us.
One: This is the inspiration of Christ's birth: that refugees and the poor are
     honored and the powerful are brought low.

All: **When we see crying needs and fail to meet them, O God, forgive us.**

One: This is the glory of Christmas: that God's love has been and always will be there for us.

All: **When we miss the vital significance of this season, open the door of the Bethlehem stable and lead us to the light.**

Time of reflection…

Words of Assurance

One: God has brought us here to witness a wonderful event:

All: **the triumph of God's love, the birth of a Savior.**

One: In that loving light, our own shortcomings fall into place and our need to begin again is clear and straightforward.

All: **We are ready to accept God's forgiveness and to make our own journey of change and reconciliation.**

One: God will bless you as you tread a fresh and faithful path.

All: **Glory and praise to God! Amen.**

Offering Prayer

One: Give thanks for God's wonderful gift in Jesus.

All: **Our gifts are a symbol of our thanksgiving; we want all people to have abundant life.**

One: Use these gifts to encourage each other,
use these gifts to care for those in need in this town/city,
use these gifts to support the mission of the wider church.

All: **We will share in the work of Jesus today! Amen.**

Commissioning

One: Do not leave your amazement at the Bethlehem stable door. Go out to change the people who wait outside!

All: **The Good News of the angels will light up a fear-filled world;**
the wonder of the shepherds will put zest in our daily routine;
the joy of the holy family will be shared with our family and friends;
the love of God, at the heart of it all, will give us and our world the courage and the hope we need!

One: You are ready for Christmas!

All: **Glory and praise to God!**

Christmas Day/Eve

Proper II (A, B, C)

Isaiah 62:6–12
Psalm 97
Titus 3:4–7
Luke2:(1–7), 8–20

Call to Worship

One: You call us to be a *holy people,* O God.

All: **We have been blessed by the coming of Jesus at Christmastime.**

One: You call us to be guided by the scriptures, the *holy book.*

All: **We have been blessed by the words of the prophets, the teachings of Jesus, and the letters of Paul.**

One: You call us to remember the stories of your faithful people, *the saints.*

All: **We have been blessed by their vision, their mission, and by their sacrifice.**

One: You call us to be faithful disciples of Jesus, your *Holy One.*

All: **We have been blessed by his humble birth, his confrontation with the evil ones, his death on a cross, and his rising to new life.**

Opening Prayer

One: We wish that Mary and Joseph had been spared the hard road to Bethlehem,

All: **but we rejoice that they endured the journey. God is with us in good times and bad!**

One: We are glad that the shepherds listened to the heavenly praise choir,

All: **and we rejoice that they found their way to the stable. God leads us to the highest good!**

One: We are not surprised that Mary thought carefully about the experience of the shepherds,

All: **and we rejoice that she treasured their words. God inspires the humble!**

One: We are one with the lowly shepherds as they return with joy to their flocks,

All: **and we too praise and glorify God. God's love is wonderful! Amen.**

Prayer of Christmas Questioning (Confession)

One: "If only the spirit of Christmas would last!"

All: **Can God's love break through, to bring an end to terror and fear?**

One: "If only the sprit of Christmas would last!"

All: **Can God's friendship be experienced, and bring the quarreling and the hostile together?**

One: "If only the spirit of Christmas would last!"

All: **Can God's generosity be influential and meet the needs of the homeless and the poor?**

One: "If only the spirit of Christmas would last!"

All: **Can God's glory be known, and move us all to return praise and prayer, thanksgiving and service, week by week?**
Time of reflection...

Words of Assurance

One: The gift of Jesus, the supreme gift of God's love, is both a call to confession and a response of action.

All: **We will ponder, with Mary, the meaning of it all, and we will resolve, with the shepherds, to leave the routine and known and risk, for the sake of God's Chosen One.**

One: God's pardon and God's active peace will be yours,

All: **and God will go with us on this new and exciting way. Thanks be to God! Amen.**

Offering Prayer

One: Loving God, you gave Jesus to a troubled world; receive our gifts.

All: **Receive with them the thanksgiving of our hearts; receive with them the dedication of our lives.**

One: May these and all our gifts bring joy to the sorrowing, peace to the troubled, power to the oppressed, and hope to the despairing.

All: **We pray in the loving Spirit of Jesus. Amen.**

Commissioning

One: We go to our homes and streets with joy!

All: **We will celebrate the birth of God's Anointed One;**
we will share with generosity God's gracious gift;
we will confront our own darkness with the light of Christ;
we will overcome the fear-makers with the peace of Christ;
we will defeat the doomsayers with the hope of Christ.

One: No one can stand in your way! You have the mind and determination of Jesus, born in Bethlehem, crucified, yet risen to eternally save!

Christmas Day/Eve

Proper III (A, B, C)

Isaiah 52:7–10
Psalm 98
Hebrews1:1–4, (5–12)
John 1:1–14

Call to Worship

One: We are the children of God.

All: God's Word has come into the world in Jesus.

One: We are the children of God.

All: God's light has enlightened the world through Jesus.

One: We are the children of God.

All: God's gracious gifts are received with Jesus.

One: We are the children of God.

All: God's love is wonderfully shown by Jesus.

Opening Prayer

One: If Mother Earth could sing out loud, she would praise God for the birth of the Savior,

All: and we would take up the song and join with heart and soul and voice.

One: If the stars and planets and galaxies could sing out loud, they would praise God for the birth of the Promised One,

All: and we would take up the song and rejoice that God's compassion was with God's people.

One: If the mountains and the rivers, the oceans and the forests could sing out loud, they would praise God for the birth of the Chosen One,

All: and we would take up the song and be glad that Jesus has come for all days and generations.

One: The children of God *can* sing out loud, and in hymns and carols and songs they praise God for the birth of Jesus at Bethlehem,

All: and the saints of every age take up the song and join their voices with ours, to bring glory and thanksgiving to our loving God. Amen.

A Prayer of Hope (Confession)

One: O God, give us light!

All: **Light in the dark places of our world: the light of refugees settled, the light of political prisoners released. Let us bring light!**

One: O God, give us light!

All: **Light in the dark places of our church: the light of strangers welcomed, the light of mission supported. Let us bring light!**

One: O God, give us light!

All: **Light in the dark places of our life: the light of new ventures begun, the light of old grudges put to rest. Let us experience light!**

One: O God, give us light!

All: **Light in the dark places of our faith: the light of doubts expressed, the light of discipleship taken seriously. Let us seek the light!**

   Time of silent reflection…

Words of Assurance

One: "The Word became flesh and lived among us…"

All: **"We have seen his glory," and that makes a difference.**

One: In the glorious light of Jesus Christ, your own priorities and those of the church fall into place.

All: **We are aware of our darkness: the darkness of self-serving, the darkness of loneliness and need ignored. But we are ready to bring the light of Christ to bear on ourselves and on our faith community.**

One: God knows joy, when light comes to the dark places! Pardon and peace are yours.

All: **Thanks be to God! Amen.**

Offering Prayer

One: O God, accept this offering, for it will bring enlightenment.

All: **The searchers will find a faithful map,**
   the sick will be aware of hope,
   the depressed will find worth in their days,
   the anxious will come to peace,
   the dispossessed will find a place to be,

One: and your people's gifts will have been blessed.

All: **Amen.**

Commissioning

One: Go from here as those who will shed the light of Christ!

All: **We will enlighten the faith-seekers;**
we will give direction to the lost;
we will stand beside the sad;
we will confront the powerful;
we will befriend the lonely;
we will advocate for those who have lost possessions or country.

One: Children of the Light, your God goes with you!

1st Sunday after Christmas

Isaiah 61:10 – 62:3
Psalm 148
Galatians 4:4–7
Luke 2:22–40

Call to Worship

One: Glory be to you, O God; you have given us joy, at this festive season.

All: Our praise rings out for Jesus, the source of Christmas joy.

One: Glory be to you, O God; you have given us salvation at this holy time.

All: Our thanksgiving is for your Chosen Child, who is our Savior.

One: Glory be to you, O God; you have given us hope at this wonder-filled time.

All: Our prayers are offered in the name of Jesus, who is come to make your purpose clear.

One: Glory be to you, O God of every age.

All: We join with hosts of saints and angels; glory be to you, O loving and eternal God!

Opening Prayer

One: O God, you were with your Chosen Child, Jesus, from the beginning;

All: from the day of our birth you have gone with us.

One: O God, you were with Jesus as he grew strong and wise;

All: as we have grown and matured, you have been our guide.

One: O God, you were Jesus when he was tempted and called;

All: in our testing times and in our life choices, you have been there.

One: O God, you were with Jesus at his life's end, at cross and rising time;

All: we believe you will be with us as our time merges with your eternal time. Glory be to you, O God! Amen.

Prayer of Confession

One: When the time of testing comes, O God,

All: strengthen us that we may be worthy of your Blessed One.

One: When the time of decision comes, O God,

All: guide us that we may choose the Way of Jesus Christ.

One: When the time of acceptance comes, O God,

All: stay with us and root out our fear.

One: When the time for speaking out comes, O God,

All: encourage us with your confident Spirit.

One: When the time for action comes, O God,

All: give us a generosity of spirit, O God, which goes way beyond our local needs.

Time of reflection...

Words of Assurance

One: It seems sometimes, O God, that we lack the courage to follow the pattern that Jesus made clear to us.

All: Then, you call us by name, affirm our ability, and set us on the road that is faithful and good. You believe in us!

One: And we set out confidently, knowing your peace in the struggle, as well as in the celebration.

All: You are there for us, O most loving God! Amen.

Offering Prayer

One: Transform the everyday through our offerings, O God.

All: Where the young doubt their abilities, give them confidence; where those of advanced years lack faith, show them the breadth of your Spirit; where the struggling are held fast in unhealthy ways, free them; where the hopeful are caught in deadening routines, revive their vision; where the lonely are despairing, encourage them to friendship.

One: And enable us to work with all our gifts to affect the transformation you have symbolized in Jesus Christ.

All: Amen.

Commissioning

One: Let your people depart in peace, O God,

All: for our eyes have seen your salvation:

One: a light, which reveals your love;

All: a holy child for every generation and race.

New Year's Day or Sunday

Ecclesiastes 3:1–13
Psalm 8
Revelation 21:1–6a
Matthew 25:31–46

Call to Worship

One: The bells ring out to welcome a new year!

All: We celebrate with joy the good times past and the memories that delight.

One: The bells ring out to welcome a new year!

All: We rejoice in the support of family and in the encouragement of our friendship circle.

One: The bells ring out to welcome a new year!

All: We celebrate practical and creative achievements and all the opportunities that lie ahead.

One: The bells ring out to welcome a new year!

All: We glory in a just and loving God, whose compassion shines from the Way of Jesus.

Opening Prayer

One: God of the past, God of the present, God of the years to come, we worship you!

All: Creator, time-maker, sustainer, source of eternal hope, we offer praise and thanksgiving to you.

One: God of the newborn, God of the exploring youngster, God of the maturing adult, we worship you!

All: Challenger, enabler, fount of wisdom, we look to you, and learn from you.

One: God of the planner, God of the artist, God of the caregiver, we worship you!

All: Source of beauty, Spirit of Compassion, friend of the oppressed, we take your Word to heart.

One: God known in Jesus, Inspiration of the prophets, Soul keeper of the saints, we worship you!

All: Holy One, focus of justice, destroyer of evil, Light in the dark places, we are ready to be activists for good.

Prayer of Confession

One: The loving God has been with you in the joys and the celebrations, the struggles and the losses of the past year; God will be with you in the year that lies ahead.

All: O God, when we are tempted to blame another person, deflect us; when we are tempted to avoid taking a decision, alert us; when we are tempted to speak ill of someone close, delay us; when we are tempted to downplay our gifts, find us opportunities to use them; when we are tempted to forget our faith, renew our journeying with Jesus; when we are tempted to keep our Christianity to ourselves, set our mind on mission; when we are tempted to hang back from bringing change, stir us to just and compassionate action.

Time of reflection…

Words of Assurance

One: You know us through and through, O God. You know when we recognize our shortcomings; you know when we gloss over our faults.

All: Give us the will to have done with those ways, those attitudes, and those words that deny our discipleship of Jesus Christ. Give us the courage to face the challenges of a new year with faithful responsibility. Give us the heart and mind of Christ.

One: With renewed resolution, God's peace will be yours!

All: Thanks be to God! Amen.

Offering Prayer

One: We offer to you, O God, our resolutions for the new year:

All: to listen more carefully to one person in our family or friendship group,
to speak out for one oppressed minority in our world;

> **to support and bring change to one community group in our
> neighborhood,**
> **to get to know and encourage one new person in this church,**
> **to grow in one aspect of our Christian faith,**
> **to think of one new way to put our faith into practice.**

One: These gifts, O God, are a token that we take our resolutions seriously. We believe that you will bless us, as we carry them out.

All: **Amen.**

Commissioning

One: With every step you take into the new year, God goes with you. God says, "Take the time to celebrate!"

All: **We say, "We will dance and laugh and sing, as we remember your gifts in creation."**

One: God says, "Take the time to forgive!"

All: **We say, "In your powerful love, there is no one who cannot be forgiven."**

One: God says, "Take the time to pray!"

All: **We say, "In our time of quiet reflection, you will speak to the most hurting and the most creative parts of us."**

One: God says, "Take time to work for justice!"

All: **We say, "We will search out the poor and the oppressed, and stand beside them."**

Epiphany

Isaiah 60:1–6
Psalm 72:1–7,10–14
Ephesians 3:1–12
Matthew 2:1–12

Call to Worship

One: A star shining in the East:

All: **discovered by those who have eyes for the unusual and the challenging.**

One: A journey into unknown territory:

All: **taken by those who have courage and curiosity.**

One: An encounter with an evil presence:

All: **evil faced yet resisted with care.**

One: The Holy One recognized, in spite of humble origin:

All: **the glory and the gifts given to God's Chosen Child.**

Opening Prayer

One: O that we had the faithfulness of the Magi!

All: **Then, God, nothing would stand in the way of our search for the highest good.**

One: O that we had the gifts of the Magi!

All: **Then, God, we would present what is appropriate to Jesus, your Anointed One.**

One: O that we had the wisdom of the Magi!

All: **Then, God, we would see the hidden threat of the evil ones and quietly avoid it.**

One: O that we had the joy of the Magi!

All: **Then, God, our encounter with Jesus would leave us exhilarated, thankful, and ready for committed discipleship.**

Prayer of Confession

One: The Magi left home and the familiar pattern of life to follow their dream.

All: **O God, reveal the star to which we aspire and enable us to follow faithfully.**

One: The Magi perceived the intentions of Herod, an evil ruler, and would not cooperate with him.

All: **O God, we will reflect on the shadowed aspects of ourselves and let the starlight of new intentions replace the darkness.**

One: The Magi, in their wealth and power, contrasted sharply with the poverty of the holy family.

All: **O God, alert us to the deep division between rich and poor and let the starlight of understanding bring sharing.**

One: The Magi were joyful when they encountered the baby Jesus, but they went home a different way.

All: **O God, give us warmth and security in the faith community and enable us to change the ways that need changing.**

Time of reflection…

Words of Assurance

One: In the light of the Bethlehem star, life changes: the way ahead shines with opportunity, dreams come to reality, choices appear, and decisions are clear before you.

All: **We will let the light of the star illumine our lifestyle, flood our spirits, and enliven our faith community.**

One: And God will bless your endeavors, grant you peace, and cherish your church.

All: **Thanks be to you, O God! Amen.**

Offering Prayer

One: Yes, these gifts will bring light, O God!

All: **The light of companionship, when journeys are taken;
the light of confidence, when evil is encountered;
the light of fulfillment, when our goal is reached;
the light of Christ, when confusion threatens;
the light of generosity, when needs come clear.**

One: Bless these gifts and bless us the givers, as we use them in our Christian service. Amen.

Commissioning

One: Go from this church as those who have seen the Bethlehem star.

All: **We will follow our most cherished dream and bring it to reality;**
we will give of our most precious gifts, to advance the Way of Jesus
Christ;
we will resist the Herods of our time, who seek to delay and
sabotage.

One: Return joyfully to your own home and proclaim by word and deed
that justice and compassion rule, and that death is eternally defeated.

1st Sunday after the Epiphany

(Baptism of Jesus)

Genesis 1:1–5
Psalm 29
Acts 19:1–7
Mark 1:4–11

Call to Worship

One: Come from the demands of everyday life, to experience peace.

All: We will experience peace as we worship the Holy One.

One: Come from the routine of everyday life, to experience community.

All: We will experience community as we support and encourage one another.

One: Come from the predictability of everyday life, to experience a challenge.

All: We will experience a challenge as we respond to the ministry of Jesus Christ.

One: Come from the uncertainty of everyday life, to experience security.

All: We will experience security as we put our trust in God, who loves us beyond limits.

Opening Prayer

One: Wonderful is your blessing of family, O God.

All: We rejoice in the joy we find among those we love.

One: Wonderful is your blessing of our daily activity, O God.

All: We rejoice in the achievement, friendship, and creativity of our day.

One: Wonderful is your blessing of our learning, O God.

All: We rejoice that there is still so much for us to find out and put into practice.

One: Wonderful is your blessing of faith, O God.

All: We rejoice that, with the Word, you inspire us and send us out to empower the oppressed and to listen to the downhearted.

One: Wonderful love is your mark, O God.

All: We thank you for its fullest expression in Jesus Christ. Amen.

Prayer of Confession

One: We gather to welcome the beginning of Jesus' ministry.

All: **Like the crowds on Jordan's bank, we come humbly, for we have much to confess.**

One: We gather expectantly, for we are ready to hear the prophetic Word.

All: **God calls us to listen carefully, plan enthusiastically, and to respond practically.**

One: We gather to make the new start that baptism symbolizes.

All: **With that Jordan crowd, we confess our fear of change, but affirm our willingness to turn our lifestyle around.**

One: We gather to witness the awesome power of the Holy Spirit.

All: **We will be inspired to renew our relationships and to work in community to enliven our neighborhood.**

Time of reflection…

Words of Assurance

One: Are you ready to change your ways:

to forgive freely,

to give of yourself with generosity,

to listen carefully,

to meet needs promptly,

to respond faithfully,

to act justly?

All: **We are ready!**

One: God's pardon and peace are yours.

All: **Thanks be to God!**

Offering Prayer

One: May the commitment we know, as members of the company of the baptized, be reflected in our offerings to you, our God.

All: **We offer our time cheerfully;**
we offer our skills and talents gladly;
we offer our money generously.

One: Bless all our gifts and put them to work in the Way of Jesus Christ, with this faith community and with communities far from this town/city.

All: **Amen.**

Commissioning

One: Go from this church with joy!

All: We have the gift of forgiveness;
   we have the Word of encouragement;
   we have the promise of God's presence;
   we have the support of the faith community;
   we have the example of Jesus in front of us.

One: Go with joy, know the peace of God in every day and in every situation.

2nd Sunday after the Epiphany

1 Samuel 3:1–10, (11–20)
Psalm 139:1–6,13–18
1 Corinthians 6:12–20
John 1:43–51

Call to Worship

One: You are here for us, O God;
All: **you give us security in an uncertain world.**
One: You encourage us to sing new songs;
All: **you joyfully set our worship free.**
One: You challenge us as we go on the journey of life;
All: **it is your gracious way that leads to fulfillment.**
One: There is no end to the love you lavish on us;
All: **we know your love is there for us, in time and beyond time.**

Opening Prayer

One: Our happiness comes through trusting God;
All: **God enables us to put life's lessons into practice.**
One: Our peacefulness comes through trusting God;
All: **God gives us calm in the midst of life's storms.**
One: Our courage comes through trusting God;
All: **with faith in God, we know a confidence that cannot fail.**
One: Our community grows through trusting God;
All: **God is present in every welcome and is known as friendship grows and deepens. Amen.**

Prayer of Confession

One: The call that comes to us to serve God is sometimes in an unexpected form.
All: **Have we been alert to the ways and people through which God's call to serve has come?**
One: The call to serve comes sometimes at an inconvenient time.
All: **Have we missed God's call because we have been busy with other activities?**

One: The call to serve God we hear clearly, but its message we fail to understand.

All: Have we checked out God's call with a trusted friend or family member?

One: The call to serve God is often a call to venture into new territory.

All: Have we the courage to break free from our self-imposed boundaries in order to serve the local and wider faith community?
Have we the courage to bring a Christian approach to our workplace and social groups?

> *Time of reflection…*

One: Living God,

All: with Samuel we reply to your call, "Speak, your servant is listening."

Words of Assurance

One: The Word of God continues to be heard.

All: In the sharpening of our listening skills,
with fresh insight into your call,
in a determination to serve faithfully,
you define our discipleship.

One: Pardon and peace are yours. Know it; believe it!

All: Thanks be to God! Amen.

Offering Prayer

One: Bless us as we work out our faith in community:

All: in our gathering together,
in our praising,
in our learning,
in our supporting,
in our speaking out,
in our keeping silent,
in our serving,
and in our giving.

One: Bless these offerings, which enliven this community of faith and faith communities far from here.

All: Amen.

Commissioning

One: What does God call us to do as we leave the church?

All: Does God call us to listen for God's call in unlikely places?
Does God call us to forgiveness, when it is the last thing we want
to do?
Does God call us to serve God's people and those who are
definitely not God's people, with compassion?
Does God call us to meet poverty and powerlessness in the Way
of Jesus?

One: Speak God! Your servants are "all ears"!

3rd Sunday after the Epiphany

Jonah 3:1–5, 10
Psalm 62:5–12
1 Corinthians 7:29–31
Mark 1:14–20

Call to Worship

One: Spirit of God moving over the waters, bringing light where there was only darkness;

All: **Holy Spirit, move among us, change us, enlighten us.**

One: Spirit of God, there at the baptism of Jesus, claiming, anointing, speaking loving words;

All: **Holy Spirit, touch us, enthuse us, claim us.**

One: Spirit of God, calling disciples in days of old and today to follow Jesus, the way, the truth, and the life;

All: **Holy Spirit, meet us, convince us, inspire us.**

Opening Prayer

One: Trust in God!

All: **God will give us the challenging task, but also the strength to get it done.**

One: Trust in God!

All: **God will call us to discipleship, and give us the insight to work out our following of Jesus.**

One: Trust in God!

All: **God will show us our role within the faith community, and sensitivity to the needs of those beside us.**

One: Trust in God!

All: **God will love us "through all the changing scenes of life," and will be there at life's end, to welcome us home. Amen.**

Prayer of Confession

One: Merciful God, we come humbly before you, for we have some tough questions to ask of ourselves.

All: **The self-giving pattern of Jesus is clear to us, dear to us; how can we ignore it so easily?**

One: In Jesus we have seen what it means to get to know a new group of people really well – surprising people, very different disciple-people.

All: **How do we react to new people and to those who are very different from ourselves in appearance and in speech?**

One: In Jesus we have seen what it means to stand with the poor and the disadvantaged, and with those who feel alone.

All: **How do we cope with the needs of persons who experience life as empty and sad?**

One: In Jesus we see what it means to resist temptation, obvious and subtle.

All: **What is our record in standing up to the pressure. Do we give in? Do we avoid? Do we go away? Or do we resist?**
Time of reflection...

Words of Assurance

One: You call us to question carefully and thoroughly, O God, and, having decided on a course of action, to commit wholeheartedly.

All: **We will not flinch from the hard choices, O God. We will do what is right, and just, and well pleasing in your sight.**

One: God goes with the faithful ones, pardon and peace are yours.

All: **Thanks be to God! Amen.**

Offering Prayer

One: These gifts are the seeds of discipleship:

All: **sown among the suffering, they will give hope;**
sown among the bereaved, they will bring the touch of comfort;
sown among the lonely, they will create links of friendship;
sown among church members, they will create a community of faith;
sown among the powerless, they will become a means to strength;
sown among the searching, they will bring wisdom.

One: God blesses these gifts as we, disciples of Jesus, seek to make them effective. Amen.

Commissioning

One: You are the rock, O God!

All: On your foundation we will be strong.

One You are the rock, O God,

All: the solid basis of our faith.

One: You are the rock, O God!

All: Our discipleship of Jesus cannot be shaken.

One: You are the rock, O God,

All: our refuge in the hard times.

One: You are the rock, O God!

All: Your steadfast love will eternally secure us.

4th Sunday after the Epiphany

Deuteronomy 18:15–20
Psalm 111
1 Corinthians 8:1–13
Mark 1:21–28

Call to Worship

One: People of faith come and worship!

All: **We rejoice in this opportunity to worship together.**

One: People of faith, come and praise!

All: **We rejoice in this opportunity to sing with heart and voice.**

One: People of faith, come and pray!

All: **We rejoice in this opportunity to open ourselves to God's leading.**

One: People of faith, come and listen!

All: **We rejoice in this opportunity to hear the scriptures and to respond with faithful service.**

Opening Prayer

One: You give us people for the times, O God.

All: **In the earliest days, you gave great leaders to Israel: Abraham, Jacob, and Moses.**

One: You give us people for the times, O God.

All: **And when a word of correction or justice was needed, you sent the prophets: Jeremiah, Amos, and Isaiah.**

One: You give us people for the times, O God.

All: **To a world crying out for salvation, your Chosen One, Jesus, came to teach, to die, and to rise again.**

One: You give us people for the times, O God.

All: **And still you send your messengers, your challengers, the agents of your love: Mother Teresa, Martin Luther King, and unsung saints we know. We thank you, O God. Amen.**

Prayer of Confession

One: You challenge us to use our faithful authority, O God:

All: **authority not reliant on the fixed pattern of the years, but on the gentle, flexible, affirming approach.**

One: You inspire us to use our faithful authority, O God:

All: **authority born of wise insight, careful study, and skillful practice.**

One: You are with us as we use our faithful authority, O God:

All: **authority rooted in Hebrew and Christian scripture, the prayer-based way of Jesus.**

One: You support us as we use our faithful authority, O God:

All: **authority which runs counter to the powerful and fear-making forces, authority that will not leave the oppressed to suffer.**

Time of reflection…

Words of Assurance

One: You know, O God, those times when we impose our opinions and our ways on others and you call us to change.

All: **We will put our rigid and selfish ways behind us; we will listen to the needs and dreams of those around us; we will search out Christ's compassionate and just way, for our faith community.**

One: As you let go your self-serving attitudes and practices, you will experience peace and fulfillment.

All: **We will! Thanks be to God. Amen.**

Offering Prayer

One: These gifts enable your faith community to sharpen its senses, God.

All: **We will be enabled to see those who struggle; we will be ready to minister to those who have suffered loss; we will hear those who cry out because they are depressed; we will be inspired to help those who don't have enough food or who live in squalor; we will gather the downtrodden together to work for the common good.**

One: You bless us and you bless our gifts, as our awareness grows. We are a grace-filled people. Amen.

Commissioning

One: Leave this church in the confidence of Jesus Christ!

All: **The faith community will be renewed;**
the sick will know hope;
the despised will get the respect they deserve;
the guilty will know pardon;
the proud will be humbled;
and each one of us will feel the loving acceptance of God.

One: Yes! You may go in peace.

5th Sunday after the Epiphany

Isaiah 40:21–31
Psalm 147:1–11, 20c
1 Corinthians 9:16–23
Mark 1:29–39

Call to Worship (Isaiah 40:28–31 altered)

One: God cares beyond our imagining;
    God has staying power that never fades;
    God gives power to the weak and strengthens the powerless.

**All: Nothing is beyond those who trust God.
    Weakness and exhaustion are facts of life;
    the young and fit eventually tire.**

One: But those who trust in God will renew their strength.

**All: Like an eagle rising in the sky, like a marathon runner at peak
    performance, nothing will stand in their way. Tiredness and
    weakness are not an option!**

Opening Prayer

One: Our times are shadowed by terror, violence, and greed.

All: Dawning Light, we praise you!

One: Our church is shadowed by uncertainty, fear, and apathy.

All: Dawning Light, we praise you!

One: Our lives are threatened by insecurity, selfishness, and change.

All: Dawning Light, we praise you!

One: Living God, Dawning Light, for our time, our church, and ourselves,

All: for the gift of Jesus, reflecting your light, we praise you. Amen.

A Prayer of Hope

One: When we experience fear, when we are downhearted and anxious,

**All: can it be that a friend, with the spirit of Jesus, will take us by the
    hand and put us back on our feet?**

One: When the world we know comes apart, when the loss of a loved one,
    the loss of a cherished dream, comes home to us,

All: **can it be that a caregiver, with the spirit of Jesus, will take us by the hand and put us back on our feet?**

One: When our faith community lacks direction, when the call to active discipleship goes unheard,

All: **can it be that a saint of today, with the spirit of Jesus, will take us by the hand and put us back on our feet?**

One: When our faith is tested, when doubts overwhelm, when your purposes seem obscure and remote, O God,

All: **can it be that a gentle teacher, with the spirit of Jesus, will take us by the hand, and put us back on our feet?**

Time of reflection…

Words of Assurance

One: In the midst of our trouble, we find ourselves spoken to by God.

All: **We will search out persons with the spirit of Jesus, who are willing to help us.**

One: When we find ourselves in a position to give confidence and support to those who are downhearted and distressed,

All: **we will not hesitate to offer them a word of encouragement and a helping hand.**

One: In receiving, you know the touch of Christ; in giving, you offer the hand of Christ. The peace of Christ will be yours.

All: **Thanks be to God! Amen.**

Offering Prayer

One: May these gifts be the means by which many persons come alive.

All: **The sick receive wholeness;**
the bereaved receive comfort;
the downtrodden find a common purpose;
the refugee finds a home.

One: Your gifts will be truly blessed, as you go with them to bring life.

All: **God be praised! Amen.**

Commissioning

One: Go from the church as committed disciples of Jesus Christ.

All: **We are ready to learn and to grow in the faith;**

we are ready to serve in the church;
we are ready to proclaim the Good News in word and deed;
we are ready to live out our Christian values and to see Christ in
those we meet.

6th Sunday after the Epiphany

(Proper 1. If this is the Sunday before Ash Wednesday,
this Proper may be replaced by the readings for
the Last Sunday after the Epiphany, Transfiguration Sunday.)

2 Kings 5:1–14
Psalm 30
1 Corinthians 9:24–27
Mark 1:40–45

Call to Worship

One: Come into the chill of our existence, O God, the cool of our soul.

All: Bring the warmth of your presence, the glow of enthusiastic worship.

One: Come into the routine of our church, O God, into the familiar nature of our relationships.

All: Bring the joy of good friends, the assurance that there are those on whom we can rely.

One: Come into our habitual ways, O God, the groove of our family life.

All: Bring the inspiration of fresh challenges, the satisfaction of caring for our loved ones faithfully.

Opening Prayer

One: O God, we rejoice that Jesus the Way goes ahead of us,

All: the pattern of our faith community, the direction of our future.

One: O God, we rejoice that Jesus the Compassionate One goes with us,

All: calling us to acts of caring, showing us how much can be achieved if we work together.

One: O God, we rejoice that Jesus the Just is there for us,

All: challenging us to confront the powerful ones, giving courage to the downtrodden.

One: O God, we rejoice that Jesus, risen and glorified, is there for us,

All: defeater of darkness, eternal promise of peace. Amen.

Prayer of Reminder (Confession)

One: You call us to do the simple things, O God, and to do them well.

All: **You remind us to care for our bodies, through a healthy diet and regular exercise.**

One: You call us to do the simple things, O God, and to do them well.

All: **You remind us to care for our minds, through a search for new truth and a determination to keep on learning.**

One: You call us to do the simple things, O God, and to do them well.

All: **You remind us to care for our souls, through the joy of regular worship, and the discipline of daily Bible reading and prayer.**

One: You call us to do the simple things, O God, and to do them well.

All: **You remind us of the teaching of Jesus, to love you, Our God, and to love our neighbor as we love ourselves.**

   Time of reflection...

Words of Assurance

One: Where we have no motivation to do the simple things well, our God will give us the resolution that we need.

All: **God will be there to encourage and to guide us.**
   God will be there to refresh us and to pick us up when we fail.

One: God will speak to you through the inspiration of friends and the witness of our faith community. Through practice and through dedication, you will see progress and know peace of mind and spirit.

All: **Thanks be to God! Amen.**

Offering

One: This is an offering that makes choice possible:

All: **the choice for peace at home and within the church,**
   the choice for justice in communities far from here,
   the choice for children where they are ignored or neglected,
   the choice for elders where they are forgotten or afraid,
   the choice for confidence where self-doubt rules,
   the choice for Christian faith where other gods prevail.

One: As courageous choices are taken, so this offering is blessed.

All: **Amen.**

Commissioning

One: Welcome the new week!

All: We welcome opportunities for bringing hope and new life:

One: hope to the suffering, new life within the neighborhood.

All: We welcome opportunities for bringing light and peace:

One: the light of Bible learning, the peace that comes with prayer.

All: We welcome opportunities for bringing friendship and encouragement:

One: the friendship of the faith community, the encouragement of one
member for another.

All: We welcome the new week with joy!

One: God goes with you into each of its days!

7th Sunday after the Epiphany

(Proper 2. If this is the Sunday before Ash Wednesday,
this Proper may be replaced by the readings for
the Last Sunday after the Epiphany, Transfiguration Sunday.)

Isaiah 43:18–25
Psalm 41
2 Corinthians 1:18–22
Mark 2:1–12

Call to Worship

One: People of God, gather to worship.

All: **We rejoice that we can offer praise and prayer.**

One: People of God, gather to listen.

All: **We rejoice that we can hear the Word of God that challenges and guides.**

One: People of God, gather in friendship.

All: **We rejoice that we can encourage and help each other.**

One: People of God, gather to serve.

All: **We rejoice that we are able to support and empower in the name of Jesus Christ.**

Opening Prayer

One: Increase our faith, O God!

All: **We believe that in Moses you showed that you care for the people you have chosen.**

One: Increase our faith, O God!

All: **We believe that in the prophets, you revealed your resistance to evil and your call to justice.**

One: Increase our faith, O God!

All: **We believe that in Jesus, you made clear your pattern of love for all time.**

One: Increase our faith, O God!

All: **We believe that your compassionate purpose is worked out by the local and worldwide community of faith. Amen.**

Prayer of Confession

One: Jesus is the teacher of the faith community.

All: Are we open to new truth?

One: Jesus brings healing through the faith community.

All: Are we ready to be a people of compassion?

One: Jesus brings acceptance to the despised and lonely.

All: Are we able to put prejudice aside?

One: Jesus brings forgiveness to the selfish and the sinful.

All: Are we ready to take time to confess openly, honestly, and thoroughly?
   Time of reflection…

Words of Assurance

One: God enables us to ask the hard questions and to face the answers that trouble us.

All: We will not hold back from the need to confess nor the need to start afresh.

One: God supports the person who recommits to the Christian way.

All: We take heart, knowing we are not alone.

One: Pardon and peace are yours!

All: Thanks be to God! Amen.

Offering Prayer

One: Bring home to us, O God, the scope of your many gifts and stir up within us the wisdom and the insight to bring change.

All: May we use this money, together with our natural talent, so that this faith community may know, and so that those touched by our mission gifts may know, that the Way of Jesus Christ is still a healing, compassionate, and wonderful way. Amen.

Commissioning

One: Your Word has made an impact on us, O God.
   We leave this church with a new attitude:

All: **ready to question, ready to doubt,**
      ready to learn, ready to pray,
      ready to commit, ready to serve,
      ready to support, ready to encourage,
      ready for discipleship, ready to confess Christ day by day.

One: You go confidently, but you do not go alone.

All: **God goes with us!**

8th Sunday after the Epiphany

(Proper 3. If this is the Sunday before Ash Wednesday,
this Proper may be replaced by the readings for
the Last Sunday after the Epiphany, Transfiguration Sunday.)

Hosea 2:14–20
Psalm 103:1–13, 22
2 Corinthians 3:1–6
Mark 2:13–22

Call to Worship (from Psalm 103)

One: God has done so much for us!

All: Bless God's holy name!

One: God has forgiven our sins!

All: Bless God's holy name!

One: God has made us whole!

All: Bless God's holy name!

One: God has crowned us with steadfast love!

All: Bless God's holy name!

One: God works with the oppressed!

All: Bless God's holy name!

One: God's goodness is from everlasting to everlasting!

All: Bless God's holy name!

Opening Prayer

One: Fill us with your love, O God!

**All: You have created us and our world; your gracious action calls us to
a loving response.**

One: Fill us with your praise, O God!

All: Your many gifts overwhelm us and call us to worship and thanksgiving.

One: Fill us with your spirit of fellowship, O God!

All: We have so much to share with our friends in the faith.

One: Fill us with your spirit of generosity, O God!

**All: We will give from our plenty and be willing to receive new visions
and fresh insights. Amen.**

Prayer of Confession

One: Encourage us to be an inclusive people, O God.

All: **When we label and exclude others, forgive us!**

One: Encourage us to be a visionary people, O God.

All: **When we are content with the old familiar ways, forgive us!**

One: Encourage us to be a compassionate people, O God.

All: **When we are reluctant to affirm or to offer a helping hand, forgive us!**

One: Encourage us to be a faithful people, O God.

All: **When we take our discipleship for granted, O God, forgive us!**

> *Time of reflection…*

Words of Assurance

One: Talk is cheap; actions speak louder than words.

All: **As we reflect on the way we think, the words we speak, and the things we do, we know that change is possible for us.**

One: God's Spirit will inspire you to act directly and positively for good.

All: **We believe that God forgives; pardon and peace will be ours. Thanks be to God! Amen.**

Offering Prayer

One: This is the action that proves our commitment, O God; this is the time when we show our discipleship is for real.

All: **Receive our offerings and bless them!**

One: These gifts will grow your compassionate and just work within this faith community and within the wider world.

All: **O God, enable people to know the Source and the Love that roots them. Amen.**

Commissioning

One: Break through your hardheartedness and indifference and forgive others.

All: **We are ready to make the effort!**

One: Break through your fixed patterns and routines and surprise others.

All: **We are ready to make changes!**

One: Break through your lack of faith and inspire others.

All: **We are ready to go forward confidently!**

One: Break through your narrow concept of faith community and embrace others.

All: **We are ready to include the whole world in our vision!**

Last Sunday after the Epiphany

(Transfiguration Sunday)

2 Kings 2:1–12
Psalm 50:1–6
2 Corinthians 4:3–6
Mark 9:2–9

Call to Worship

One: In the beauty of a snow-covered forest, sparkling with sunlight;
    in the beauty of a fast flowing stream, sparkling with sunlight;

All: **Artist and Creator God is revealed to us.**

One: In the smile of a newborn baby, in the love of parents for their child,

All: **vulnerable, miraculous, and in family, God is revealed to us.**

One: In the laughter of children on the school bus, in joy-filled evenings in
    the park, at the rink,

All: **friendly, enthusiastic, and happy God is with us.**

One: In the silence of a meditating moment, in the quiet of an evening
    prayer,

All: **gently, confidently, God's will comes clear to us.**

Opening Prayer

One: Take us to the mountaintop, O God; we will see things differently.

All: **We will see the great faith figures of the past and value their influence.**

One: Take us to the mountaintop, O God; we will be amazed.

All: **We will see your Beloved One, Jesus, and know he has words for us
    to hear.**

One: Take us to the mountaintop, O God; we will be awed and afraid.

All: **We will know the mystery of The Holy and be ready to worship.**

One: Bring us down from the mountaintop, O God, and prepare us for
    service.

All: **We will go about the saving work of Jesus in our church, in this
    neighborhood, and in our suffering world. Amen.**

Prayer of Confession

One: Loving God, you can transform the everyday routine.

All: **You can transform the ordinary with fresh insights and new ways of looking at people we know.**

One: You can transform the faith community.

All: **You can transform the church through rededicated leaders and a burning desire to make the gospel come alive around us.**

One: You can transform each one of us.

All: **You can transform us through a willingness to acknowledge our flaws, but also to accept our hidden talents and to put them to work in Christ's service.**

One: You can transform our world.

All: **You can transform the world through a series of small steps to promote peace, justice, and freedom, which start with us and with our faith community.**

Time of reflection…

Words of Assurance

One: God of the rushing wind, God of the still small voice, you will speak to us:

All: **words to banish fear,**
words to conquer sin,
words to renew our faith,
words to set us free,
words to set us on the right path again.

One: As you listen, as you determine to go with God, as you know God with you, pardon and peace are yours.

All: **Thanks be to God! Amen.**

Offering Prayer

One: You have known us in the high moments of life, O God, and you are with us when life is tough and the journey is adventurous; we bring our gifts to you.

All: **Bless our offering as it is used to meet needs compassionately;**
bless our offering as it is used to raise up the downhearted;
bless our offering as it is used to give a new vision;
bless our offering as it brings the value of young persons before us.

One: Jesus blessed people in these ways.
All: **We are his disciples. Amen.**

Commissioning

One: Transform us, O God!
All: **Transform our apathy into a willingness to get involved.**
One: Transform our nearsightedness into a broad vision,
All: **a vision that takes account of those far beyond family and friends.**
One: Transform our critical nature;
All: **enable us to see the essence of all that is challenging and joyful in others.**
One: Transform our faith,
All: **from a narrow set of beliefs, to a questioning, continuous, and practical quest.**
One: With the spirit of Christ you will be transformed!

Lent 1

Genesis 9:8–17
Psalm 25:1–10
1 Peter 3:18–22
Mark 1:9–15

Call to Worship

One: We go with Jesus into the wilderness.

All: We feel the need to get away to reflect and to pray.

One: We stay with Jesus in the wilderness.

All: We sense the power of the Tempter calling us to the easy, self-serving way.

One: We endure with Jesus in the wilderness,

All: aware of a Supportive Presence showing us a faithful way, a compassionate path.

One: We return with Jesus from the wilderness,

All: renewed in body, mind, and spirit, ready to be about God's work.

Opening Prayer

One: Prepare us for our Lenten journey, O God;

All: give us the courage to venture into the challenging places of heart and spirit.

One: Come with us on our Lenten journey, O God;

All: strengthen us that we might learn and grow as disciples of Jesus Christ.

One: Join us with others on our Lenten journey, O God;

All: in faithful solidarity, we will search out dark forces of oppression and defeat them with the light of Jesus Christ.

One: Be with us at the end of our Lenten journey, O God;

All: that at the foot of the cross we might look up and understand your wonderful love. Amen.

Prayer of Confession

One: Lent is a good time to look carefully at our patterns of life and faith in your presence, O Most Understanding God.

All: **Where we have followed the path of deception, change our direction.**

One: You will change our direction.

All: **Where we have not taken the feelings of others into account, give us sensitivity.**

One: You will give us sensitivity.

All: **Where we have hung back from working for the common good, bring us back into fellowship.**

One: You will engage us in faith community.

All: **Where we have ignored the practice of prayer and forsaken the Word, faithfully renew us.**

One: You will renew us.

All: **Where we have missed opportunities to stand with the powerless, give us courage.**

One: You will give us courage.

Time of reflection…

Words of Assurance

One: God hears your silently offered prayers and stands ready to bring you a fresh start as members of the family of God.

All: **We will renew our faith and practice; we will begin again with joy and determination.**

One: God stands ready to help you as you rededicate yourself to the Christian way. Pardon and peace are yours!

All: **Thanks be to God! Amen.**

Offering Prayer

One: These are our gifts, O God, offered to bring change in the Way of Jesus Christ.

All: **Through these gifts, selfishness will be questioned, humility nurtured, and compassion fostered. Through these gifts, justice will be promoted, community strengthened, and the gospel proclaimed.**

One: Bless them, and bless all who receive them, for Jesus is at the heart of them.

All: **Amen.**

Commissioning

One: You challenge us to reflect and serve, O God.

All: **Give us honesty in our looking back;**
give us generosity in our relationships;
give us hope in the midst of turmoil;
give us energy to take on faithful endeavors;
give us patience when all does not go according to plan;
give us endurance as we walk the testing Lenten path.

One: Go with God; God goes with you. Peacefully, securely, God goes with you!

Lent 2

Genesis 17:1–7, 15–16
Psalm 22:23–31
Romans 4:13–25
Mark 8:31–38 or Mark 9:2–9

Call to Worship

One: Covenant God, God of Abraham and of Sarah, we come before you.
All: **You will keep your word!**
One: Covenant God, God of Amos and of Jeremiah, we come before you.
All: **You will keep your promises!**
One: Covenant God, God of the New Covenant in Jesus, we come before you.
All: **The cross is your trusted sign!**
One: Covenant God, God whose love is sealed in the waters of baptism, we
come before you.
All: **Your covenant endures!**

Opening Prayer (based on Mark 8:31–38)

One: We stand with the disciples and listen to Jesus;
All: **we cannot believe that God's Chosen One must suffer.**
One: We reflect with the disciples;
All: **there has to be another way, a way of compromise.**
One: Then, Jesus foretells his death and we are stunned;
All: **we agree with Peter: "Jesus you have got it wrong!"**
One: The heart-wrenching truth comes home to us;
All: **as followers of the Jesus Way, we are called to share the sacrificial path. O God, give us the courage to stay faithful! Amen.**

Prayer of Confession

One: Christ's conscious decision was to walk the tough but faithful road to
Jerusalem.
All: **In our decision making, O God, save us from compromising the Christian Way.**

One: The community of disciples failed Jesus when the pressure was on.

All: **In our striving to be a faithful community, O God, save us from putting self-interest first.**

One: Pilate gave Jesus a way out, a way to avoid the cross.

All: **In our temptation to walk away from responsibility, O God, keep the cross in front of us.**

One: "Father, forgive them," said Jesus, as he hung dying.

All: **When we are reluctant to have done with past wrongs, O God, enable the words of Jesus to become our word.**

Time of reflection...

Words of Assurance

One: Jesus will go to Jerusalem!

All: **In the light of Jesus' dedication to the way of faith, the obvious and the subtle temptations come clear to us.**

One: With God's loving power for you, with you, in you and through you, there is no failure of nerve that cannot be overcome, no sin that cannot be forgiven.

All: **With God's loving power behind us and before us, assuring us and securing us, the new way opens up, the dead ends are finished.**

One: Pardon and peace are yours.

All: **Thanks be to you, our God! Amen.**

Offering Prayer

One: At this Lenten time, we reflect on the hard choices Jesus made. May these gifts reflect our choice of the Christian Way:

All: **a way of compassion,**
a way of healing,
a way of support for the powerless,
a way of thanksgiving and worship,
a way of love.

One: Bless these gifts, O God, as you have blessed us with the gift of Jesus Christ. Amen.

Commissioning

One: Summon up your courage; Jesus is calling you to follow the difficult but faithful path.

All: **We will resist temptation, resist the easy way out;**
we will reflect carefully on our areas of testing;
we will search out the Way of Jesus thoroughly, carefully;
we will find strength with our fellow travelers along the way;
we will follow the Way, courageously, faithfully, even sacrificially!

One: Rejoice in God's loving presence, with you continually.

Lent 3

Exodus 20:1–17
Psalm 19
1 Corinthians 1:18–25
John 2:13–22

Call to Worship

One: Into our comfortable ways, O God,

All: breathe vigorous reflection.

One: Into our ordered ways, O God,

All: breathe lively innovation.

One: Into our worldly ways, O God,

All: breathe hints of holiness.

One: Into our self-seeking ways, O God,

All: breathe the notion of sacrifice, that we may walk the Lenten walk with Jesus, calmly, purposefully, and without fear. Amen.

Opening Prayer

One: Jesus took the hard road that led to Jerusalem.

All: We give thanks, O God, that we too can take the faithful way.

One: The disciple friends of Jesus were with him on that journey.

All: We give thanks, O God, for the friends who stay with us in the testing times.

One: Jesus was prepared to confront the evil ones of his day.

All: We give thanks, O God, for those who speak out against power and injustice today.

One: Jesus could face the cruel cross because you were with him.

All: We give thanks, O God, that in our Lenten challenges you are there – a rock, a leader, and the promise of eternal love. Amen.

Prayer of Confession

One: There is an anger of prejudice that keeps us from listening to another person's point of view.

All: **Give us, O God, a willingness to listen, even when we disagree with what is being said.**

One: There is an unexpressed anger that keeps feelings and emotions buried within.

All: **Give us, O God, the confidence to reveal those sentiments we find most difficult to put into words.**

One: There is an anger that masks our own insecurity and doubt.

All: **Give us, O God, a faithful confidence that allows us to believe in ourselves, as you believe in us.**

One: There is a selfish anger that will not share in the neighborhood and with the needy worldwide.

All: **Grant us, O God, a generosity of spirit that will share with those whose need is great, but whose names we may never know.**

Time of reflection…

Words of Assurance

One: Give us, O God, the insight that enables us to know the difference between rage and heartfelt, justified anger.

All: **Give us, O God, the willingness to reflect on those feelings of anger that are ours. Enable us to express our anger straightforwardly and constructively.**

One: Bless us with those who are able to receive our hard feelings,

All: **both as an individual and as a member of the faith community.**

One: By dealing with your feelings of anger, peace will be yours.

All: **Thanks be to God! Amen.**

Offering

One: We seek God's blessing on our gifts.

All: **We will experience God's blessing as compassionate needs are met, as the distressed are supported, as the lonely find a friend, and as the call to justice is heard. Amen.**

Commissioning

One: Are you ready to follow the challenging way of Jesus Christ?

All: **We will choose between justice and injustice;**
we will speak out and act for what is right;
we will the experience the disapproval of those who want only a
quiet life;
we will conquer our fear;
we will feel the weight of the cross.

One: You are ready!

Lent 4

Numbers 21:4–9
Psalm 107:1–3, 17–22
Ephesians 2:1–10
John 3:14–21

Call to Worship (from Psalm 107)

One: God is good; God's steadfast love lasts forever.

All: We know it, we believe it, we proclaim it!

One: God is good; God's steadfast love lasts forever.

All: Those who thirst for new life are satisfied; those who hunger for the living Word are filled!

One: God is good; God's steadfast love lasts forever.

All: The imprisoned ones know freedom; sinners know pardon!

One: God is good; God's steadfast love lasts forever.

All: The powerful are humbled; the needy are raised up from their distress!

One: God *is* good!

All: God's steadfast love lasts forever!

Opening Prayer

One: You are with us as we go with Jesus towards Jerusalem, most gracious God, and we are thankful.

All: You stay with us in the tough moments of reflection and confession.

One: You are with us, reminding us of all that sustains us as a faith community,

All: our common life of faith, our encouragement of one another.

One: You are with us as we make clear your realm of love and justice beyond this church.

All: You are our inspiration for mission; you are at the heart of our service to others.

One: You are with us as we walk beside the cross-carrying Jesus.

All: You remind us of the demanding call to discipleship, of our need to confront the dark, self-serving powers.

One: Most gracious God,

All: stay with us! Amen.

A Prayer of Listening

One: "God so loved the world that he gave his only son, that everyone who has faith in him may not die, but have eternal life."

All: **When we are ready to affirm our own worth and to use our hidden talents, we hear the words...**

One: "God so loved the world..."

All: **When we find the faithful strength to forgive the person who has caused us harm or heartache, we hear the words...**

One: "God so loved the world..."

All: **When our church can focus its gaze on those most despised, most ignored in our society, we hear the words...**

One: "God so loved the world..."

All: **When our world leaders are prepared to reduce resource use for the sake of future generations, we hear the words...**

One: "God so loved the world..."

Time of silence...

Words of Assurance

One: Eternal life begins as you are willing to use your hidden talents and to forgive those who have harmed you.

All: **Eternal life for the church begins as we show concern for the oppressed, for those for whom Christ died.**

One: Eternal life for our planet begins when our leaders look beyond our present day needs to the needs of our children and grandchildren.

All: **"God so loved the world" that God gave us Jesus Christ.**

One: Pardon and peace are yours.

All: **Thanks be to God! Amen.**

Offering Prayer

One: You, O God, know the consequences of our giving; you know the results of our generosity.

All: **They will be found in persons supported, sickness faced, hope restored, the helpless given aid, the oppressed finding a will and a way to defeat the oppressor.**

One: As change takes place for good, our gifts will be blessed and you will smile on us, the givers.

All: **Amen.**

Commissioning

One: O Love that will not let us go, you will go with us.

All: O Love that will not let us go, bear with us when we ignore you.
O Love that will not let us go, forgive us when we turn our backs on crying needs.
O Love that will not let us go, do not leave us when we leave others to work out their own salvation.
O Love that will not let us go, we see the cross on the hill and we know that whatever comes, you will go with us!

Lent 5

Jeremiah 31:31–34
Psalm 51:1–12 or Psalm 119:9–16
Hebrews 5:5–10
John 12:20–33

Call to Worship

One: You will be our God, and we will be your people.

All: **In times of weakness, in moments of temptation, the covenant holds.**

One: You will be our God, and we will be your people.

All: **When the journey is rough, when friends let us down, the covenant holds.**

One: You will be our God, and we will be your people.

All: **In our struggle to be a faithful community, in the uncertainty of faithful endeavors, the covenant holds.**

One: You will be our God, and we will be your people.

All: **In our work for justice, in our response of worship, the covenant is proved. You will be our God, and we will be your people.**

Opening Prayer

One: You welcome us, O God, as travelers along the highway of faith.

All: **We have set out in hope and we believe you are with us on the way.**

One: The end of this Lenten season brings home the challenge of the journey.

All: **But you, O God, have given us the person of Jesus Christ, to trust and to follow.**

One: Jesus says "The hour is come," the cross stands menacingly at the end of the road.

All: **We will not look back; we will confront the self-serving powers of darkness.**

One: Love Crucified reveals a wonderful new prospect.

All: **Death is not the end; the Way goes on beyond the cross; Love is eternal. Amen.**

Prayer of Confession

One: Tell us, Jesus, why were you crucified?

All: **I was crucified for speaking out against political leaders.**
I was crucified for standing with the poor.
I was crucified for treating children and women as equals.

One: You would be "crucified" today, Jesus!

One: Tell us, Jesus, for whom did you care especially?

All: **I cared for the mentally sick and the physically challenged.**
I cared for those who had socially shunned diseases.
I cared for widows.
I cared for those who had lost loved ones.

One: Your care is still needed!

One: Tell us, Jesus, what did your followers find difficult?

All: **They found it difficult to understand my close relationship with God.**
They found it difficult to come to terms with my death.
They found it difficult to believe that life and hope can arise from dead ends.

One: Jesus, nothing has changed!

One: Tell us, Jesus, do you have some words for your church?

All: **"The people honor me with their lips, but their hearts are far from me."**
"Do not judge and you will not be judged, do not condemn and you will not be condemned."
"Father, forgive them, they do not know what they are doing."

One: We will try to be faithful!
Time of reflection…

Words of Assurance

One: The past is left in the past. The crowds are cheering. The time of repentance and new life is here!

All: **We are ready to make amends. We are ready for a fresh start. We are ready to look at our lives and our church life, in the light of Christ.**

One: The past is left in the past. The palm branches are waved. The time of confidence, the time for change, has arrived!

All: **Nothing can stop us now! Not opposition, not crucifixion. We will live by the Word of God. Christ is our Risen Promise!**

One: In Christ you have nothing to fear. Peace is yours!

All: **Praise to Christ's name! Amen.**

Offering Prayer

One: The coming sacrifice of Christ calls us to wonder about the effectiveness of our gifts.

All: **Will our worship speak to the needs of the coming generation?**
Will reconciliation arise out of conflict?
Will we move from self-interest to concern for others?
Will we see the faith community as a priority for ourselves and for our neighborhood?
Will we move out to address the needs of a troubled world?

One: Time will tell, but we are committed to keeping the cross before us – a symbol and a measure of what we can achieve in Christ.

All: **Amen.**

Commissioning

One: Go from the church joyfully!

All: **We stand with the crowd and feel the excitement of Jesus coming into the city.**

One: Go from the church in solidarity with your friends!

All: **We mingle with the disciples and sense the significance of the occasion, the foretaste of a testing time ahead.**

One: Go from the church determined!

All: **We look towards the cross-hill and know that God's love is more than a match for all that lies ahead.**

Lent 6

Palm/Passion Sunday

LITURGY OF THE PALMS
Mark 11:1–11 or John 12:12–16
Psalm 118:1–2, 19–29

LITURGY OF THE PASSION
Isaiah 50:4–9a
Psalm 31:9–16
Philippians 2:5–11
Mark 14:1 – 15:47 or Mark 15:1–39, (40–47)

Call to Worship (Option 1, the Palms)

One: Jesus, God's Chosen One, is here! Encourager of the weak, opponent of evil, advocate for justice.

All: **"Hosanna!"**

One: Jesus, God's Chosen One, is here! Promised by the prophets, friend of the poor, teacher of the disciples.

All: **"All blessed is the One who comes in the name of the Lord!"**

One: Jesus, God's Chosen One, is here! Comrade of the oppressed, sign of God's presence, freedom-bringer.

All: **"Blessed is the coming kingdom of our ancestor David."**

One: Jesus, God's Chosen One, is here! Son of Joseph and Mary, peace-creator for Zacchaeus, God's Love in action.

All: **"Hosanna in highest heaven!"**

Call to Worship (Option 2, the Passion)

One: Joy is ours; the exultant crowds welcome Jesus.

All: **Sorrow is ours; we know the crowds will cry out, "Crucify him!"**

One: Joy is ours; the disciples are caught up with enthusiasm for their leader.

All: **Sorrow is ours; the disciples will desert their leader at his moment of need.**

One: Joy is ours; we sense the power of evil on the run.

All: **Sorrow is ours; we realize the huge cost, which is symbolized by the cross.**

Opening Prayer (Option 1)

One: Proof of your love: you took the Jerusalem road, and would not be put off when friends suggested an easier way.

All: Jesus, we will be supportive in your faith community.

One: Symbol of your love: the crowds scattered their palms and hailed you as their royal hero.

All: Jesus, we recognize your worth and will serve with enthusiasm.

One: Tortured in your love: you did not give in when you were abused, insulted, and hung on the cross.

All: We are humbled when we "survey the wondrous cross."

One: Triumph of your love: the cross stands empty, as the tomb will be.

All: Jesus, we realize that death will not have the last word, not now, not ever. Amen.

Opening Prayer (Option 2, Holy Communion)

One: Eternal God, your love is with us as we celebrate the coming of Jesus into Jerusalem:

All: crowds cheering, palms waving, the disciples enthusiastic.

One: Your love stays with us as we slink away afraid,

All: when the cheering is silenced, when the palms are trampled, and when the sound of nailing is heard.

One: Your love becomes a personal love, a love for our faith community,

All: as bread is broken, wine is poured out, and Jesus is graciously remembered. On this glorious, painful day, fill us with your love! Amen.

Prayer of Confession

One: We listen to the crowds, at first cheering and enthusiastic, then crying, "Crucify him! Crucify him!"

All: We recognize our own changing loyalties; the ease with which we can be swayed.

One: We listen to the few words of Jesus before the ones in power; we feel his awesome presence.

All: We recognize how you, O God, can keep us strong at the time of testing.

One: We listen to the compassionate response of Jesus on the cross, to the thief beside him.

All: **We recognize how difficult it is for us to respond sensitively and appropriately to need.**

Time of reflection...

Words of Assurance

One: God, we are overwhelmed and humbled by your gift of Jesus Christ to us.

All: **We will respond to your supreme gift with honest reflection, renewed commitment, and firm resolve.**

One: Pardon and peace will be ours.

All: **Thanks be to God! Amen.**

Offering Prayer

One: Sorrow and joy mingle in our offering, O God.

All: **As we rejoice in the triumphant entry of Jesus, we celebrate the effectiveness of our gifts, which are the means of healing, the symbols of compassion, the way of the gospel, the sign of hope.**

One: (As we share bread and the cup,) we sorrow in the needs of our world:

All: **the plight of the poor, the despair of the depressed, the self-serving power of money, the power of the evil ones.**

One: Bless our gifts, O God, that palm and cross may renew us in the service of Jesus Christ. Amen.

Commissioning

One: Blessed is the one who comes in the name of the Lord!

All: **Hosanna! We will open our hearts to his faithfulness.**

One: Blessed is the one who comes in the name of the Lord!

All: **Hosanna! We will stand beside those who are crucified today.**

One: Blessed is the one who comes in the name of the Lord!

All: **Hosanna! We will work with those who bear his name.**

One: Blessed is the one who comes in the name of the Lord!

All: **Hosanna! We will thank God for our Savior, Jesus Christ.**

Holy Thursday

Exodus 12:1–4, (5–10), 11–14
Psalm 116:1–2, 12–19
1 Corinthians 11:23–26
John 13:1–17, 31b–35

Call to Worship

One: You call us to serve one another, O God,

All: to serve joyfully, and freely.

One: You call us to serve one another, O God,

All: to serve without counting the cost.

One: You call us to serve one another, O God,

All: to serve when we would rather be served.

One: You call us to serve one another, O God,

All: to serve as followers of Jesus, the Servant.

Opening Prayer

One: Jesus took the bowl and the towel and washed the dirt of the day away.

All: We come before you, loving God, to make a fresh start.

One: Jesus took the bowl and the towel and met the needs of his friends
with compassion.

**All: We come before you, loving God, remembering the ties of family
and friendship.**

One: Jesus took the bowl and towel and shared himself with his disciples.

**All: We come before you, loving God, as part of a faith community that
accepts and shares.**

One: Jesus put away the bowl and the towel and reminded his friends that
they were called to serve.

**All: We come before you, O God, prepared to search out the focus and
pattern of our Christian service. Amen.**

Prayer of Confession

One: You have called us to serve, O God, and we are questioning our service. Have we served you in our words, attitudes, and actions: to friends, family, and neighbors?

All: **Speak, O God, for your servants are listening.**

One: Have we served you within the faith community: its worship life, its teaching and care of others, its outreach into the neighborhood?

All: **Speak, O God, for your servants are listening.**

One: Have we served you in the wider world: in our willingness to be involved in political or union action; in our readiness to stand with the poor, the sick, the challenged, and with those who are denied justice?

All: **Speak, O God, for your servants are listening.**

Time of reflection…

Words of Assurance

One: You speak, O God, and we hear your voice.

All: **It comes through trusted friends,**
through the challenge of newspapers and television news programs.
It comes as we reflect on the Hebrew and Christian scriptures.
It comes through the messages we hear in church.
It comes through meditation and prayer.

One: As you respond to God's voice, pardon and peace are yours.

All: **Thanks be to God! Amen.**

Offering Prayer

One: It is through the use of all our gifts that we faithfully serve, O God. Accept and bless these.

All: **We will serve you, with our praise and our prayer.**
We will serve you, as we serve those who are afraid.
We will serve you, as we give hope to the suffering.
We will serve you, as we stand beside the dejected.
We will serve you, in our gifts to those whose names we do not know, but whose needs are great.

One: God will accept your gifts of time, talent, and money.

All: **And we will rejoice! Amen.**

Commissioning

One: Go from here as servants of The Servant.

All: We will look out for the needs of our friends and meet those needs.

One: Go beyond your circle of friends!

All: We will look out for the needs of our faith community and work with others.

One: Go beyond your faith community!

All: We will look out for the oppressed in our city/town, and work with other faith groups to bring change.

One: Go beyond your city/town!

All: We will look out for the struggling in our world and find ways to support them.

One: And people will know that you are servants of The Servant.

Good Friday

Isaiah 52:13 – 53:12
Psalm 22
Hebrews 10:16–25 or Hebrews 4:14–16, 5:7–9
John 18:1 – 19:42

Call to Worship

One: The suffering servant, despised and rejected.

All: **We remember Jesus, despised by those for whom he was the voice of conscience, rejected even by his friends.**

One: The suffering servant, a man of sorrows and acquainted with grief.

All: **We remember Jesus, who empathized with those the world treated harshly and who gave hope to the bereaved.**

One: The suffering servant, wounded for our transgressions.

All: **We remember Jesus, who paid the ultimate price for the self-interest and will for control that is mirrored in our nature.**

One: The suffering servant, led like a lamb to the slaughter.

All: **We remember Jesus, for whom a refusal to compromise or to submit to corrupt leaders led inevitably to a cross and death. We fall silent in the face of his sacrifice.**

Time of reflection…

Opening Prayer

One: The shadow of the cross falls on us as we worship;

All: **we lift our eyes to see Jesus, condemned by the powerful.**

One: The shadow of the cross falls on us as we worship;

All: **humiliation and mocking by the soldiers has been the lot of Jesus.**

One: The shadow of the cross falls across us as we worship;

All: **on the cross is written, "Jesus of Nazareth, King of the Jews." What irony! Jesus is the one to whom we give our loyalty.**

One: The shadow of the cross falls across us as we worship;

All: **Jesus is supported at this agonizing time by his mother and by two other women, but by only one disciple.**

One: The shadow of the cross falls across us as we worship;

All: **we fall silent in the face of his sacrifice.**

Time of reflection…

Prayer of Confession

One: Nailed to the cross,

All: by those who put self-interest above principles. People like us!

One: Put among thieves,

All: by those who were afraid of risking change. People like us!

One: Humiliated in public,

All: by those whose eyes were closed to the needs of the poor. People like us!

One: Shunned at this crucial moment,

All: by those who would not see the significance of his sacrifice. People like us!

Time of reflection…

Words of Assurance

One: The cross, symbol of sacrifice:

**All: evil persons confronted,
self-seeking groups challenged,
loving community tested,
comfortable traditions questioned.**

One: Sacrifice calls for sacrifice!

All: As you grace us with the commitment of your Sacrificed One, O God, the right choices will be made, peace will be ours, and we will go forward renewed and unafraid. Amen.

Commissioning

One: Christ has been crucified; the terrible work has been done.

**All: Compassion has been ended;
the powerless have been abandoned;
the leaders are smiling smugly;
the religious ones are sighing with relief;
the followers are scattered.**

One: But (the sun is rising behind the cross-hill)
bread has been broken, the cup has been shared.

All: Quietly, confidently, thankfully, we await resurrection.

Easter Sunday

Acts 10:34–43 or Isaiah 25:6–9
Psalm 118:1–2, 14–24
1 Corinthians 15:1–11 or Acts 10:34–43
John 20:1–18 or Mark 16:1–8

Call to Worship

One: Defeater of death!
All: **Christ is risen!**
One: Creator of community!
All: **Christ is risen!**
One: Way of hope!
All: **Christ is risen!**
One: Promise of wholeness!
All: **Christ is risen!**
One: Christ is risen!
All: **Christ is risen indeed!**

Opening Prayer

One: The stone has been removed from the tomb;
All: **the power of death is at an end.**
One: The grave clothes have been abandoned;
All: **fear and hesitation are over.**
One: The Risen Christ is encountered (in the garden);
All: **the community of faith will be restored.**
One: Christ is once more with his friends;
All: **hope is alive, new horizons beckon, oppression and injustice are shattered. Amen.**

Prayer of Confession

One: We have seen the face of the Risen Christ.
All: **We have seen the face of the Risen Christ: bewildered, angry, despairing, among those who have suffered loss.**
One: Where we have failed to recognize Christ,

All: **forgive us!**

One: We have seen the face of the Risen Christ.

All: **We have seen the face of the Risen Christ: worried, unsure, lacking confidence, downhearted, among those close to us.**

One: Where we have failed to recognize Christ,

All: **forgive us!**

One: We have seen the face of the Risen Christ.

All: **We have seen the face of the Risen Christ: not welcomed, searching, unchallenged, in our faith community.**

One: Where we have failed to recognize Christ,

All: **forgive us!**

One: We have seen the face of the Risen Christ.

All: **We have seen the face of the Risen Christ: discouraged, powerless, defeated, among the disadvantaged of our world.**

One: Where we have failed to recognize Christ,

All: **forgive us!**

Words of Assurance

One: All-loving God, you know us through and through. You encourage our acts of careful reflection and renewed commitment.

All: **As we recognize the face of Christ in our family members, in our friends, and in the stranger, so you give us the will to be with them, as we would be with Jesus.**

One: As you know Jesus Christ and walk with him, pardon and peace are yours.

All: **Thanks be to God! Amen.**

Offering Prayer

One: What would you give for an empty tomb?
What would you give for a Risen Savior?
What would you give for a restored community?
What would you give for a gospel that endures?

All: **We gave nothing; it was graced to us.**
Bless these offerings, O God, for through them, the spirit of the Risen Christ is at work in our day and generation. Amen.

Commissioning

One: The stone has been rolled away;

All: the power of death is broken.

One: The stone has been rolled away;

All: the ties of community have been restored.

One: The stone has been rolled away;

All: God's love shines out triumphantly.

One: The stone has been rolled away;

All: The Risen Christ fills us with Easter hope.

2nd Sunday of Easter

Acts 4:32–35
Psalm 113
1 John 1:1 – 2:2
John 20:19–31

Call to Worship

One: Strengthen our faith at this resurrection time, O God;

All: give us the courage of Mary Magdalene.

One: Strengthen our faith at this resurrection time, O God;

All: give us the honesty of Thomas the apostle.

One: Strengthen our faith at this resurrection time, O God;

All: give us the joy of the gathered disciples.

One: Strengthen our faith at this resurrection time, O God;

All: give us the active spirit of the Risen Christ. Christ be praised. Alleluia!

Opening Prayer

One: The Risen Christ will transform us!

All: Christ will transform our earthbound worship into an act of glorious praise.

One: The Risen Christ will transform us!

All: Christ will transform our hesitant community into an active, enthusiastic group of friends.

One: The Risen Christ will transform us!

All: Christ will transform our fear of the unknown into a ready spirit of adventure.

One: The Risen Christ will transform us!

All: Christ will transform our self-serving into service of those around us, and of those whose crying needs are brought home to us. Amen.

Prayer of Confession

One: Like the soldier at the foot of the cross, we do our duty and good people get hurt.

All: Give us the common sense, O God, to question those ways that go against our conscience and your spirit of love.

One: Like Pilate in his palace, we are quick to put the responsibility for our decisions on someone else.

All: Give us the courage, O God, to stand firm for what is right and to accept the responsibility that is ours alone.

One: Like Peter in the courtyard, we are ready to deny the highest part of ourselves, if there are going to be unpleasant consequences.

All: Give us the wisdom, O God, to avoid the easy way that leads to guilt which does not go away.

One: Like Thomas in the upper room, we doubt the fact that Jesus is risen.

All: Give us the Easter strength, O God, to accept our doubts as stepping stones towards a more honest and dynamic faith.

Words of Assurance

One: You accept the whole range of our falling short, O God, and you give us eyes to see its significance. Give us also the will to learn from our failure and the resolution to make a fresh start, in the spirit of the Risen Christ.

All: Christ be praised!

One: Your sins are forgiven; peace is yours.

All: Alleluia! Thanks be to God! Amen.

Offering Prayer

One: Living God, accept these gifts, and the reasons we give them:

**All: to bring purpose where there is hesitancy,
to bring courage where there is struggle,
to bring comfort where there is loss and bereavement,
to bring assurance where there is self-doubt,
to bring justice where there is oppression.**

One: These are the gifts of new life!

All: Amen.

Commissioning

One: Confident that the Risen Christ is with us, we leave this community of the faithful.

All: **Renewed in the Spirit, we will encourage the doubting.**
Renewed in the Spirit, we will encourage the apathetic.
Renewed in the Spirit, we will encourage the downhearted.
Renewed in the Spirit, we will encourage those who lack hope.
Renewed in the Spirit, we will be servants and advocates for
Jesus Christ.

3rd Sunday of Easter

Acts 3:12–19
Psalm 4
1 John 3:1–7
Luke 24:36b–48

Call to Worship

One: God's Word calls us to thanksgiving.

All: **"Give thanks to God; God is good, God's love is eternal."**

One: God's Word calls us to praise.

All: **"Praise God! All who serve God, all who worship in the Lord's house."**

One: God's Word calls us to community in faith.

All: **"How wonderful it is, how pleasant for God's people to live together in harmony."**

One: God's Word calls us to freedom and justice.

All: **"God hears the groans of the prisoners, and sets free those who were doomed to die."**

Opening Prayer

One: Surprise us, O most glorious God!

All: **Surprise us with your message of hope, when the world seems a hostile place.**

One: Surprise us, O most caring God!

All: **Surprise us with your sustaining presence, when we do not know where to turn.**

One: Surprise us, O most challenging God!

All: **Surprise us with your way of justice and truth, when the easy way beckons.**

One: Surprise us, O most revealing God!

All: **Surprise us with the face of Jesus Christ, in the most unexpected of persons. Amen.**

Prayer of Confession (based on Luke 24)

One: Join us on our Easter journey, Risen and Blessed One.

All: Refresh our memory and remind us of our shortcomings as your followers.

One: Join us in the upper room, Risen and Blessed One.

All: Enable us to put our fears and doubts in the past, and to greet you with joy.

One: Join us as we (come to the table) work together, Risen and Blessed One.

All: Remove the limits from our vision and open us up to new opportunities, new horizons.

One: Join us in a renewed community, Risen and Blessed One.

All: Give us enthusiasm as we serve faithfully, and courage to proclaim the Good News.

    Time of reflection...

Words of Assurance

One: You are with us, O God, as we reflect on our lives in the light of Jesus:

All: his strength while being rejected,
his need for good and understanding friends,
his willingness to confront the power structures,
his insistence on following the truth rather than the easy way,
his close, prayerful bond with you.

One: God is with you as you resolve to think, speak, and act in a faithful way. God wants you to have a fresh start.

All: Pardon and peace will be ours! Thanks be to you, forgiving God! Amen.

Offering Prayer

One: You bless our gifts, O God, and you bless us as we encounter your Word.

All: You bless us with enlightenment;
you bless us with a will to make a difference;
you bless us with a generous spirit.

One: As we are blessed, so we become a blessing to others within this community of faith.

All:　**As we are blessed, so we are freed to give support to those far beyond this community, in mission and in service. Amen.**

Commissioning

One:　The risen spirit of Jesus is with us as we leave this church:
renewing our worship,
binding us in Christian community,
encouraging us to use our varied gifts,
calling us to stand up and be counted.

All:　**In the spirit of Christ, everything is possible!**

One:　Fear and death are defeated.

All:　**Alleluia!**

4th Sunday of Easter

Acts 4:5–12
Psalm 23
1 John 3:16–24
John 10:11–18

Call to Worship (reflecting Psalm 23)

One: Calm is your gift to us, O God.

All: You lead us on the right path.

One: In the valley of the shadow,

All: you take our hand.

One: As we sit at table,

All: you join us and secure us.

One: You are eternally good for us,

All: and eternally present with us.

Opening Prayer (Option 1)

One: God loved the world and gave Jesus for us.

All: For that gift above all others, we give God thanks.

One: God loved the world and showed us compassion in Jesus.

All: God calls us to notice and to share with the needy as Jesus did.

One: God loved the world and made truth come alive in Jesus.

All: We have in Jesus a teacher to whom we will listen and from whom we will learn.

One: God loved the world and we should love one another in Christ.

All: "This is the way the world will know that we are his disciples, if we show love for one another." No other way! Amen.

Opening Prayer (Option 2, Christian Family Sunday)

One: A baby smiles and gurgles,

All: and we give thanks to God for the gift of life and for the wonder of human growth.

One: A family plays ball in the front yard,

All: and we give thanks to God for love that binds a family together.

One: A couple exchange memories on the front porch,

All: **and we give thanks to God for the joy that is ours in family over the years.**

One: Three generations share a pew together in church,

All: **and we give thanks to God for the faith that has supported and inspired our family life. Amen.**

Prayer of Confession (Option 1)

One: When we feel useless and despairing,

All: **you lead us from the dark valley, O God, and you give us our confidence back.**

One: When we have no wish to join in, but try to go it alone,

All: **you lead us back to community, O God, and you show us the joy and the satisfaction of working with others.**

One: When we refuse to meet a challenge or to get involved in a just cause,

All: **you lead us from the place of denial, O God, and you give us the courage to stand with the oppressed.**

One: When we neglect our life of faith and cannot find time for worship, prayer, or your Word;

All: **you lead us back into faithfulness, O God, and you enable us to see our priorities as disciples of Jesus Christ.**

Time of reflection…

A Prayer of Encouragement for Families (Option 2)

One: When the ties of family or relationship become strained,

All: **help us, O God, to express our feelings and to listen carefully to each other.**

One: When the times of illness or hard testing are upon us,

All: **help us, O God, to renew our faith and to know that you are with us.**

One: When we are faced with a crucial decision,

All: **help us, O God, to share our options and concerns, and to go forward with confidence.**

One: When stress or depression get the better of us,

All: **help us, O God, to search out the persons who can help and who can fill us with your Easter hope.**

Time of reflection…

Words of Assurance

One: God will not leave you without power or control; God will lead you into the way of new life.

All: **We take courage from the promises and actions of God as we have read about them, believe them, and experience them.**

One: God will grant you a fresh start; pardon and peace are yours!

All: **Thanks be to God! Amen.**

Offering Prayer

One: Jesus promised us abundant life, O God, and our response is to give abundantly in return; you have given so much for us!

All: **We present our gifts for blessing:**
so those who are without direction will find the Way of Jesus,
so those who are suffering will know the compassion of Jesus,
so those who are alone will link up with the friends of Jesus,
so those who are afraid will find peace in the community of Jesus.

One: These gifts will be blessed as we follow the Good Shepherd and as we care for his flock.

All: **Amen.**

Commissioning (Option 1)

One: You know us by name, O God, and your care for us is beyond all understanding. You will go with us as we leave the church.

All: **In the paths of joy, you will celebrate with us.**
When hardship and testing are our lot, you will endure with us.
When we are separated from your way or your people, you will bring us back. When our time passes into your time, your eternal love will come home to us.

One: Compassionate God, you are always with us! You will never leave us.

Commissioning (Option 2, Christian Family Sunday)

One: May the Father of the human family go with us and sustain us in our family life.

All: **May the Mother of the church family go with us and nurture our common life together.**

One: May the Parent of all humankind go with us and show us how closely related we have become.

5th Sunday of Easter

Acts 8:26–40
Psalm 22:25–31
1 John 4:7–21
John 15:1–8

Call to Worship

One: Jesus is the true vine and God is the vine grower.
All:　**We are the branches.**
One: It is God's Word that makes the branches strong;
All:　**and the Word bears fruit.**
One: The Word gives rise to action;
All:　**and action proves our discipleship.**
One: God celebrates when we act faithfully;
All:　**and we give back praise and glory, to God.**

Opening Prayer

One: Where do we see you, O God?
All:　**We see you in the most helpless baby, as creator and caregiver.**
One: When do we know you, O God?
All:　**We know you in the laughter and play of growing children, as the spirit of carefree joy.**
One: How do we experience you, O God?
All:　**We experience you in mature men and women, as the renewer of confidence and strength for a new day.**
One: In whom do we know you, O God?
All:　**We know you in those of later years, as the provider of unforeseen opportunities and the eternal sign of hope. Amen.**

Prayer of Confession

One: We look for your acceptance and forgiveness, Loving God.
All:　**We have been slow to trust, yet quick to criticize.**
　　　We have been reluctant to give, yet ready to take advantage.

We have known the words to say, but have kept them to ourselves.
We have been challenged to bring change, but have failed to get started.
We have been aware of the opportunity to witness to our faith,
but have let the moment pass.
And we are conscious of those times, O God, when we have denied
the way of integrity and compassion shown to us by Jesus Christ.

  Time of reflection…

Words of Assurance

One: God will not leave us without hope. The graceful gift of Jesus is proof
positive of that "blessed assurance."

All: We are accepted by God.

One: God will enable us to express our troublesome thoughts and memories.

All: We are forgiven by God.

One: God will give us confidence to speak of new things, to work in new
ways, and to cooperate with new people.

All: We are renewed by God.

One: Pardon and peace are yours!

All: Thanks be to God! Amen.

Offering Prayer

One: These offerings are blessed by you, our Loving God,

**All: as the distressed find a friend,
as the despairing find hope,
as the church links arms with its faith neighbors,
as the Good News of Jesus Christ is heard and celebrated,
as the faith community makes an impact locally, and as it reaches
out to touch the wider world. Amen.**

Commissioning

One: O most loving God, you are there for us:

**All: You are strength, in tough times; you are comfort, in times of loss;
you are a challenge, in apathetic times; you are faith, in doubting
times; and you are Love, for us and with us – an integral part of us, at
all times.**

One: Go with us as we return to the world this morning.

6th Sunday of Easter

Acts 10:44–48
Psalm 98
1 John 5:1–6
John 15:9–17

Call to Worship (from Psalm 98)

One: The whole of planet Earth is singing as we come to worship God.

All: **Birds are dawn-chorusing, bees are humming, and elephants are trumpeting. Seas are roaring, rivers are applauding, hills are singing a chorus of joy.**

One: God's steadfast love and faithfulness is for us and for all people.

All: **And so the orchestras are performing, the jazz bands are jamming, the choirs are harmonizing, and the groups are "out of sight."**

One: God has done marvelous things!

All: **And the singing will never be done; never ever be done.**

Opening Prayer

One: Friends of God, you are called to praise and prayer.

All: **It is our joyful and thankful response to God's goodness.**

One: Friends of God, you are called to hear the Word:

All: **the Word that instructs, the Word that challenges, the Word that reveals the teachings of Jesus Christ.**

One: Friends of God, you are called into faith community:

All: **a community that encourages, a community that brings out talent, a community that works in harmony.**

One: Friends of God, you are called to a far reaching vision:

All: **a vision beyond the local church, even beyond the boundaries of the nation.**
Our giving and our service will honor the name of Jesus. Amen.

A Prayer of Intention

One: This is Christ's commandment: "love one another as I have loved you."

All: **When we take the time to listen and to explain, we reveal that love.**

One: This is Christ's commandment: "love one another as I have loved you."

All: When we help or support another person, at a personal cost to ourselves, we reveal that love.

One: This is Christ's commandment: "love one another as I have loved you."

All: When we share in community our talent, our enthusiasm, and our will to work for the common good, we reveal that love.

One: This is Christ's commandment: "love one another as I have loved you."

All: When we reject the values of the selfish, when we confront the powerful, we reveal that love.

Time of reflection…

Words of Assurance

One: Christ alive for us,

All: hope revived for us,

One: strength renewed in us,

All: love pardoning us,

One: Christ's peace surrounding us,

All: this joyful Easter time.

Offering Prayer

One: Loving God, you are the source of all blessing.

All: Alert us to your generosity and in love enable us to return the blessing.

One: Bless those whose needs are great; in our families, in our community, in our church, and in our troubled world.

All: We pray in the name of Jesus, who is a blessing to us. Amen.

Commissioning

One: Love is all you need!

**All: The love of a potter for her craft, the love of a sailor for the open water,
the love of a mother for her child, the love of a child for a puppy,
the love of a teacher for his class, the love of a nurse for her patients,
the love of a grandpa for his grandchildren, the love of Christ for his disciples,
the Love of God for us, God's children.**

One: Love *is* all you need!

7th Sunday of Easter

Acts 1:15–17, 21–26
Psalm 1
1 John 5:9–13
John 17:6–19

ASCENSION OF THE LORD
Acts 1:1–11
Psalm 47 or Psalm 93
Ephesians 1:15–23
Luke 24:44–53

Call to Worship

One: We are happy to be here, O God,

All: to be with our faithful friends in our church home.

One: We are happy to be here, O God,

All: to share in the singing and to listen to your Word.

One: We are happy to be here, O God,

All: to find inspiration for our daily living and purpose in our service of others.

One: We are happy to be here, O God,

All: to remember your faithfulness in Jesus Christ and his death on the cross for us.

Opening Prayer

One: Testify! Tell the world what God has done!

All: God has created our world and has given us lakes and mountains, stars and wonder as we look up at the night sky.

One: Testify, for God has given us more!

All: God has given each of us life and breath, and has put us in families and among friends.

One: Testify, for God has been faithful!

All: God has given us the ancient leaders and the prophets, has spoken through the scriptures, and has formed the faith community.

One: Testify, for God has held nothing back!

All: **God has sent Jesus Christ for us and for all people. In Christ's birth, God's care was made clear; in his baptism, God's vocation was revealed; and in his death on the cross, we understand just how far God will go.**

Prayer of Dedication (Confession)

One: In a world where many are dedicated to attaining power over others,

All: **we dedicate ourselves to peace and to the support of the downtrodden.**

One: In a church where many find it easier to keep the traditional ways,

All: **we dedicate ourselves to fresh expressions of worship and to innovative ways of service.**

One: In a friendship circle where many experience relationships on a superficial level,

All: **we dedicate ourselves to listening carefully and to going the extra mile.**

One: In our families where it is difficult to keep priorities straight in a fast moving world,

All: **we dedicate ourselves to taking time for each family member and to enjoying the moment with them.**

   Time of reflection...

Words of Assurance

One: To get our feelings sorted out, to get our relationships in harmony and our actions right, we need to rededicate ourselves to you, O God.

All: **Through our prayers, through the inspiration of scripture, and through the guidance of your saints of today, we will become your renewed and faithful people.**

One: And God will bless your endeavors and grant you peace.

All: **Thanks be to God! Amen.**

Offering Prayer

One: O God, creative and caring, just and giving, receive the gifts we bring;

All: to create,

to care,

to free,

to promote justice,

and to share your goodness with the world. Amen.

Commissioning

One: May we be one, O God!

All: One in openness to the truth,

one in the acceptance of people who are "different,"

one in the joy of worship,

one in responsibility for the faith community,

one in our willingness to resist evil,

one in our sharing with other faiths,

one in our mission and service to the wider world,

one in our discipleship of Jesus Christ.

Pentecost Sunday

Acts 2:1–21 or Ezekiel 37:1–14
Psalm 104:24–34, 35b
Romans 8:22–27 or Acts 2:1–21
John 15:26–27, 16:4b–15

Call to Worship
One: Holy Spirit, come amongst us!
All: **Inspire our worship, strengthen our faith.**
One: Holy Spirit, stay with us!
All: **Deepen our fellowship, support our sharing.**
One: Holy Spirit, challenge our discipleship!
All: **Encourage us to venture out, give us the compassion of Jesus.**
One: Holy Spirit, work through us!
All: **Touch the downhearted with hope, move the dispirited with Love.**

Opening Prayer
One: Soaring, flowing, questing, dancing,
All: **the Holy Spirit leads us to praise.**
One: Searching, finding, changing, challenging,
All: **the Holy Spirit calls us to faithfulness.**
One: Gently, calmly, simply, persistently,
All: **the Holy Spirit invites us to reflection.**
One: With perseverance, with encouragement, with joy, with urgency,
All: **the Holy Spirit moves us to action. Come, Holy Spirit, and be with us, now and always! Amen.**

A Prayer of Questioning/Confession (from Acts 2)
One: "A sound like the rush of a violent wind…"
All: **Do we doubt the power of God's Spirit to move us and our faith community for good?**
One: "Divided tongues as of fire…"
All: **Could the power of God's Spirit set us on fire with enthusiasm for worship and for work, in our church and in our neighborhood?**
One: "And how is it that we hear…in our own native language…"

All: Have we realized that the Word of God has universal truth, universal potential to empower the rejected and downtrodden?

One: Peter quotes the prophet Joel: "I will pour out my Spirit upon all flesh…"

All: Are there no limits to the loving influence of God? Is it possible that saint and sinner, rich and poor, can all be touched and changed by God?

Time of reflection…

Words of Assurance

One: Living God, your Spirit will radically change us.

All: Into our apathy, your Spirit breathes enthusiasm;
within our uncertainty, your Spirit forms faith;
into our hardness of heart, your Spirit breathes compassion.

One: Know the peaceful power of the Spirit around you,
the pardoning power of the Spirit for you,
the graceful power of the Spirit setting you free.

All: Thanks be to God! Amen.

Offering Prayer

One: We believe that your Holy Spirit will go to work through these offerings, O God,

All: as the weak find support,
as the vulnerable gain confidence,
as the disabled get fair treatment,
as the disillusioned can dream again.

One: We pray in the name of Jesus, who strengthens.

All: Amen.

Commissioning

One: The Holy Spirit will go to work within each one of you and within this faith community.

All: The Spirit calls us, and we are encouraged to respond faithfully.
The Spirit moves us, and we are encouraged to work diligently.
The Spirit fills us, and we are encouraged to live peacefully.
The Spirit challenges us, and we are encouraged to act with justice.
The Spirit loves us, and we are encouraged to mirror that love,
every day and in every way.

Trinity Sunday

1st Sunday after Pentecost

Isaiah 6:1–8
Psalm 29
Romans 8:12–17
John 3:1–17

Call to Worship

One: Gracious God, Creator of the universe, source and giver of love,

All: we worship you.

One: Jesus Christ, Chosen One of God, defeater of evil, founder of faith
community,

All: we are your disciples.

One Holy Spirit, Inspiration to the world, influence for good, hope for the
future,

All: we will work with you.

Opening Prayer

One: Come to us quietly, gently, O God.

All: Enable us to hear your still small voice as we pray.

One: Come to us in all the wonder and diversity of creation, O God.

All: Enable us to respond with heartfelt praise and thanksgiving.

One: Come to us in the person of Jesus and his saints of the ages, O God.

All: Enable us to follow with faith and responsibility.

One: Come to us through the inspiration of the Holy Spirit, O God.

All: Enable us to bring light to the dark places. Amen.

Prayer of Affirmation (Confession)

One: We have heard the word from God to the prophet Isaiah: "Who shall I
send and who shall go for us?"

**All: Some say, "We are feeling the weight of our years." Others say,
"We haven't the necessary experience." But the reply comes,
"Here am I, send me!"**

One: "Who shall I send and who shall go for us?"

All: Some say, "We are not team players." Others say, "We have so much to learn about the faith." But the reply comes, "Here am I, send me!"

One: "Who shall I send and who shall go for us?"

All: Some say, "We cannot take on the fear making powers of the world." Others say, "The influence of evil is all pervasive." But the reply comes, "Here am I, send me!"

Time of reflection…

Words of Assurance

One: In spite of your hesitations and doubts,

All: **in spite of our evasions and feelings of weakness,**

One: you have heard the call from God.

All: **We have heard the call and we know there is work to be done.**

One: There is work to be done among your family and friends,
there is support to be given among the disadvantaged and powerless.

All: **We will reply, with Isaiah, "Here am I, send me!"**

Offering Prayer

One: John writes, "God so loved the world that he gave his only Son."

All: **Our gifts pale in comparison with that Gift among gifts.**

One: Accept our offerings, loving God, that as followers of your Anointed One, we may change our faith community and our small corner of the world, in the way and in the spirit of Jesus Christ.

All: **We will take up this glorious challenge! O God, bless our endeavors. Amen.**

Commissioning

One: Go from this church as those who have experienced a new birth!

All: **Reborn to confidence, we will use our hidden talents.**
Reborn to responsibility, we will respond to crying need.
Reborn to faith, we will learn and serve readily.
Reborn to community, we will work carefully with others.
Reborn in Christ, we will enjoy and share his love.
Reborn to hope, we will never be afraid.

Proper 4 [9]

Sunday between May 29 and June 4 inclusive (if after Trinity Sunday)

1 Samuel 3:1–10
Psalm 139:1–6, 13–18
  or Deuteronomy 5:12–15 and Psalm 81:1–10
2 Corinthians 4:5–12
Mark 2:23 – 3:6

Call to Worship

One: As the summer breeze blows, as the water runs clear and free,
All: we respond to God the Creator, "Here I am, for you called me."
One: In the midst of family, for a situation where suffering is confided,
All: we respond to the Compassionate God, "Here I am, for you called me."
One: Within our faith community, as we offer our worship, as we pledge our service,
All: we respond to our God of the Church, "Here I am, for you called me."
One: Meeting the anxiety of a good friend with words of hope,
All: we respond to the Ever-Present God, "Speak, Lord, for your servant is listening."

Opening Prayer

One: Glorious God of the seventh day, we worship you!
All: This is the day for praise in God's house; this is the day when we come together as God's people.
One: Glorious Sunday God, we worship you!
All: This is the day to put stress and daily anxieties behind us as we focus on your Word for us.
One: Glorious Sabbath God, we worship you!
All: This is the day for us to listen and to get ready for the tasks of mission and service that lie ahead for us.
One: God of the seventh day, God of *all the days*, we worship you!
All: Each day we will learn about the Way of Jesus; each day we will respond to the downhearted as committed disciples of Christ. Amen.

Prayer of Confession

One: You know us through and through, O God.

All: **You come to us in the straightforward, challenging words of a friend.**

One: There is no time when you are not present to us, O God.

All: **You are there as we face the most far reaching decision; your voice speaks to us through our conscience.**

One: Sometimes we wish you did not care so completely, O God:

All: **when we take the selfish path, when we choose the darkness rather than the light.**

One: You go with us in the challenging times, O God.

All: **You are there as we venture out and as we take risks that reflect our Christian calling.**

Time of reflection…

Words of Assurance

One: You, O God, will never let us down; you go the distance with us.

All: **Into our hesitancy and lack of resolution, breathe strength of purpose, O God.**

Into our wavering sense of direction, breathe your faithful Way, O God.

And mark our renewed lives with the blessing of your peace. Amen.

Offering Prayer

One: We take your creative goodness to us so much for granted, O God. It seems like diamonds in an old battered box.

All: **As we offer you our treasure, give us the wisdom to recognize how we fall short of your wonderful generosity.**

One: God will use your gifts for God's compassionate and encouraging purposes.

All: **We offer them fully and freely, and we offer ourselves to make them effective.**

One: God will accept your gifts and bless them.

All: **Praise and thanks to God! Amen.**

Commissioning

One: Your God will not keep a score of wrongs.

All: Our loving God will not harbor grudges.

God will open us to new endeavors and will help us to confront the darkness that binds us, and the apathy that saps our strength. God will enable us to have done with the past that holds us back.

One: Tomorrow is a new day. Go into that day with confidence and hope!

Proper 5 [10]

Sunday between June 5 and June 11 inclusive (if after Trinity Sunday)

1 Samuel 8:4–11, (12–15), 16–20, (11:14–15)
Psalm 138
　　　or Genesis 3:8–15 and Psalm 130
2 Corinthians 4:13 – 5:1
Mark 3:20–35

Call to Worship

One: We are ready, O God; we wait for your blessing.

All:　From the experiences of another week, we come to you.

One: We wait for your blessing.

All:　From the twists and turns of friendship, we come to you.

One: We wait for your blessing.

All:　From our encounters with temptation, we come to you.

One: We wait for your blessing.

All:　From our efforts to follow Christ, we come to you.

One: We wait for your blessing.

All:　And you will bless us, O God, in this our morning worship.

Opening Prayer

One: We are strong, as disciples of Christ!

All:　We gain strength as we learn and apply the teachings of Jesus.

One: We are compassionate, as disciples of Christ!

All:　We look to those who confess the Way of Jesus, and who heal, and comfort, and listen.

One: We confront the powerful, as disciples of Christ!

All:　We are not intimidated by position, influence, money, or threats.

One: We are faithful, as disciples of Christ!

All:　We have a life of prayer; we seek to build up a faith community following the example of Jesus. Amen.

A Prayer of Reassurance

One: Though our dreams and ambitions are delayed,

All:　we will not lose heart! God gives us hope.

One: Though our health suffers, our loved ones hit hard times,

All: we will not lose heart! God gives us endurance.

One: Though our faith community is tested and struggling,

All: we will not lose heart! God gives us the Spirit's power.

One: Though life itself is limited and uncertain,

All: we will not lose heart! God gives us the joy of eternity.

> *Time of reflection...*

Words of Assurance

One: If we can trust you, O God, we have nothing to fear.

All: We will trust you to go with us, as we risk and venture;
to stay with us, when the hard times come;
to work with us, in community;
to be with us, when our time merges with your time.

One: As you trust, so God's peace is your peace.

All: Thanks be to God! Amen.

Offering Prayer

One: Gifts for the world we bring!

All: These gifts will find a home among refugees and among those
searching for dignity and survival.

One: Gifts for our church we bring!

All: These gifts will find a home among those who are suffering,
tested, and alone.

One: Gifts for ourselves we bring!

All: These gifts will come home to us, as we grow in the faith,
grow in our discipleship, and find joy in worship.

One: God will bless your gifts.

All: And we will be blessed! Amen.

Commissioning

One: Family of God, go faithfully from this place!

All: We will give support to our family members who are challenged and afraid.
We will be companions to church members on difficult personal journeys.
We will seek to understand and help local, national, and global
communities facing hard times.

One: Your family *is* God's family.

Proper 6 [11]

Sunday between June 12 and June 18 inclusive (if after Trinity Sunday)

1 Samuel 15:34 – 16:13
Psalm 20
     or Ezekiel 17:22–24 and Psalm 92:1–4, 12–15
2 Corinthians 5:6–10, (11–13), 14–17
Mark 4:26–34

Call to Worship (from Psalm 20:7)

One: Some people trust in influence and in who they know.
All: **We trust in the power of a loving God.**
One: Some people trust in money and in property.
All: **We trust in the power of a loving God.**
One: Some people trust in health that does not falter.
All: **We trust in the power of a loving God.**
One: Some people trust in a life without an ending.
All: **We trust in the power of a loving God.**

Opening Prayer

One: So many different sorts of people are gathered to worship you, O God:
All: **different in age and in outlook, different in background and in occupation, together in giving thanks.**
One: We have so many different feelings as we gather to worship you, O God:
All: **downhearted and lacking confidence, worried and depressed, together in hope.**
One: We have so many different ways of following Jesus, as we gather to worship you, O God:
All: **practical and compassionate, spiritual and prayerful, together as disciples.**
One: We have so many different visions for the faith community, as we gather to worship you, O God:
All: **focusing on the local community, witnessing through music, serving the global church, together in Christ's love. Amen.**

A Prayer for Growth from Small Beginnings (Confession)

One: As in the seed there is the potential for growth and wonderful change, so we think of the change that one small act may bring to life:

All: a church member advertises a meeting to found a hospice for the dying.

One: We think of the change that one small act may bring to life:

All: a fellow worker with an addiction is put in touch with a 12-step group.

One: We think of the change that one small act may bring to life:

All: a bereaved person without cooking skills is given his first lesson by a neighbor.

One: We think of the change that one small act may bring to life:

All: facing a major decision, we find a trusted friend who listens without judging.

> *Time of reflection...*

Words of Assurance

One: We put no limits on your power to help us for good, O God.

All: You will take our small beginnings and make more of them than we could ever imagine.

One: As we increase our faith in you, loving God, increase our faith in ourselves, that we may achieve more than we could ever dream, or hope, or aspire to.

All: Then we will know the peace of God, which passes all understanding. Thanks be to God! Amen.

Offering Prayer

One: You have chosen us as givers, O God, and also those who work with the gifts of the faith community. Bless us in this work!

All: May the generosity of our gifts of money be matched by our willingness to give our time and talents to Christ's present-day work.

One: Within the church and beyond its walls there is much to do.

All: We are committed to this faithful work; we will not be discouraged!

One: God will go with you! Amen.

Commissioning

One: No longer afraid, we go forth with joy!

All: The love of God will motivate and direct us.

One: Filled with hope, we go forth with praise on our lips!

All: The example of Jesus Christ will show us the way.

One: Held in the love of God, we go forth to bring change for good!

All: We will be inspired to work with God's Holy Spirit.

Proper 7 [12]

Sunday between June 19 and June 25 inclusive (if after Trinity Sunday)

1 Samuel 17: (1a, 4–11, 19–23), 32–49 and Psalm 9:9–20
    or Job 38:1–11 and Psalm 107:1–3, 23–32
    or 1 Samuel 17:57 – 18:5, 10–16 and Psalm 133
2 Corinthians 6:1–13
Mark 4:35–41

Call to Worship

One: God never fails us;

All: **in the testing times, God is there.**

One: God gives us strength;

All: **in our moments of weakness, God is there.**

One: God is our companion;

All: **when we feel alone, God is there.**

One: God is to be trusted;

All: **when we do not know where to turn, God is there.**

Opening Prayer

One: In our strength and in our weakness, we worship you, O God.

All: **You will use us when we are strong and support us when we are weak.**

One: In our youth and in our mature years, we worship you, O God.

All: **You are with us in laughter and in play when we are young; you give us wisdom as we grow old.**

One: In our doubting and in our faith, we worship you, O God.

All: **You will inform our doubts and confirm us in our Christian faith.**

One: In our reflection and in our service, we worship you, O God.

All: **You are present as we pray and you are the selfless spirit behind our care for others. In all the contrasts and changes of life, we worship you, loving God! Amen.**

A Prayer for Peace in the Midst of Life's Storms

One: When the moment of turmoil comes out of nowhere,

All: you, O God, are the voice of calm, the touch that reassures.

One: When the varied stresses of life combine to overwhelm us,

All: you, O God, enable us to set our priorities and to get back on a steady course.

One: When the encouragement of family and the support friends fails us,

All: you, O God, will give us confidence to search out other sources of help.

One: When the storm hits home at our faith community,

All: you, O God, will provide us with the endurance we need and the hope of better days ahead.

> *Time of reflection…*

Words of Assurance

One: Comfort and sustain us, O God, in the midst of life's storms. Empower us with the patience and the faithful pattern of Christ in the coming days.

All: In Christ, the fear and the panic melts away, replaced by faithfully firm resolve. The storms and the darkness no longer hold us in their grip.

One: Thank God. You are released, you are free!

All: Amen.

Offering Prayer

One: These offerings are our means of serving you, loving God.

All: Through them ministry is maintained;
through them, the scriptures are studied and the gospel is proclaimed;
through them, the poor are lifted up and the downhearted are encouraged;
through them, the faith community comes alive;
through them, the living Christ is encountered.

One: Bless these gifts and the time and the skills that go with them.
Bless them in the name of Jesus, your Anointed One.

All: Amen.

Commissioning

One: May the peace of God be *your* peace as you leave this church:

All:　**peace in the midst of struggle,**
　　　peace in the midst of despair,
　　　peace when the hard times hit home,
　　　peace when there is conflict in family,
　　　peace when there is ill will between friends,
　　　peace when the church is a quarrel zone,
　　　peace when world events bring terror;

One:　the peace of God, which calls for insight, hard work, and endurance;
　　　the peace of God, which at the end of the day passes all understanding.

Proper 8 [13]

Sunday between June 26 and July 2 inclusive

2 Samuel 1:1, 17–27 and Psalm 130
    or Wisdom of Solomon 1:13–15, 2:23–24
    or Lamentations 3:23–33 and Psalm 30
2 Corinthians 8:7–15
Mark 5:21–43

Call to Worship

One: Touch us with your presence, O God!

All: We will respond with worship that is joyful and free.

One: Touch us with your presence, O God!

All: We will hear the Word, spoken for us and for our faith community.

One: Touch us with your presence, O God!

All: We will experience the revealing, healing, power of the Spirit.

One: Touch us with your presence, O God,

All: and we will be your compassionate presence to others.

Opening Prayer of Thanksgiving

One: For your creative glory, which shines from every flowing stream and sings out from every bird,

All: we give you thanks, most gracious God.

One: For the joy that is ours at work, within the family circle, and when we relax with our friends,

All: we give you thanks, most gracious God.

One: For your presence in the rough and tumble of life and when the pressure is on,

All: we give you thanks, most gracious God.

One: For the peace of Christ which this faith community extends, as it reaches out to our town/city, and to communities far from here;

All: we give you thanks, O most gracious God. Amen.

Prayer of Confession

One: We search for a way that is faithful to your vision, O God.

All: Into our uncertainty, into our lack of resolution, you breathe confidence.

One: We search for a way that is faithful to the Way of Jesus, O God.

All: **Into our lack of trust, into our half-hearted discipleship, you breathe faithfulness.**

One: We search for a way that secures us when we feel afraid, O God.

All: **Into our moments of darkness, into our discouragement and fear, you breathe reassurance.**

One: We search for a way that gives us fulfillment in faith community, O God.

All: **Into our loneliness, into our hope that we can make it on our own, you breathe the joy of friendship.**

One: We search for a way that makes a difference in the world, O God.

All: **Into our frustration of "What can one person do?" you breathe purpose and small effective actions.**

Time of reflection…

Words of Assurance

One: In confidence we come before you, O God.

All: **You will affirm us;**
you will direct us;
you will encourage us;
you will deepen our friendships;
you will give us global responsibility.

One: And we will know the peace that comes from faithful living.

All: **Thanks be to God! Amen.**

Offering

One: God of all our giving and all our receiving, bless this offering.

All: **Enable us to *give* in a just and compassionate spirit, and enable us to *receive* with dignity and with thankfulness. Amen.**

Commissioning

One: Go forth as a blessed and forgiven people!

All: **We have been nourished through our worship and we are joyful!**
We have been challenged by God's word and we are hopeful!
We have been gathered in faith community and we are strengthened!
We are sent out into the world and we will be effective!

One: Christ encourages you, God secures you, the Holy Spirit inspires you!

Proper 9 [14]

Sunday between July 3 and July 9 inclusive

2 Samuel 5:1–5, 9–10 and Psalm 48
    or Ezekiel 2:1–5 and Psalm 123
2 Corinthians 12:2–10
Mark 6:1–13

Call to Worship

One: Be confident; hold your heads up high!

All: God's glorious presence is with us.

One: Be confident; rejoice in solidarity!

All: God's Word will strengthen us.

One: Be confident; face the unknown future!

All: God is present for us, in time and beyond.

One: Be confident; be ready for action!

All: God has entrusted us to do God's work.

Opening Prayer

One: A baby opens her eyes to the world for the first time,

All: and we open our hearts to our loving God in worship.

One: A butterfly opens its wings in the sunshine for the first time,

All: and we open ourselves to see God's creation in a whole new light.

One: A young child goes through the school gates for the first time,

All: and we open ourselves to looking at Jesus in completely new ways.

One: A newly qualified nurse finds herself on the hospital ward for the first time,

All: and we open ourselves to serving as disciples of Jesus with an enthusiasm we had never imagined. Amen.

A Prayer of Discipleship (Confession)

One: Jesus called his disciples to follow wholeheartedly.

All: We are reluctant to give our Christian discipleship priority in our lives.

One: Some of the disciples saw Jesus only as a prophet or holy man.

All: We often shape the person of Jesus into our image of him.

One: Jesus entrusted the disciples with exactly the same healing and evil-facing work he carried out.

All: We will find that this same work awaits us today.

One: When the pressure was on in Jerusalem, at the trial and crucifixion of Jesus, the disciples were nowhere to be seen.

All: **We tend to back off and to go in the other direction when our faithful words or actions come under attack.**

> *Time of reflection...*

Words of Assurance

One: These can be moments to shape us as followers;

these can be moments of fresh insight;

these can be moments of determination;

these can be the moments when peace breaks through.

All: **If we seize the moment, O God, we will experience your pardon and follow the discipleship way – the Way of Jesus Christ. Amen.**

Offering Prayer

One: This is the faith community that nurtures us and gives us hope:

All: **our familiar and well-loved...(name of your church)...Church. May these gifts strengthen and encourage members and friends!**

One: The...(mission/community fund)...is the way in which...(name of your denomination)...makes the influence of Jesus Christ known, beyond the local church and community.

All: **May these gifts bring justice, promote compassion, inspire fellowship, and empower the powerless. Be with us as we use all our gifts, O God. Amen.**

Commissioning

One: You are the chosen ones of Christ; commit yourselves to serve!

All: **In the midst of the downhearted, we will bring hope.**

Where people try to get by on their own, we will bring them into faith community.

For the troubled and distressed, we will bring a compassionate presence.

Where values are centered on self, we will bring sharing.

In times of darkness and disillusion, we will bring the light of Christ.

One: In Christ's service you will discover yourself.

Proper 10 [15]

2 Samuel 6:1–5, 12b–19 and Psalm 24
        or Amos 7:7–15 and Psalm 85:8–13
Ephesians 1:3–14
Mark 6:14–29

Call to Worship

One: With song and dance,
All: we worship God.
One: With heart and mind,
All: we worship God.
One: With joy and enthusiasm,
All: we worship God.
One: With our works as well as our words,
All: we worship God.
One: In the heart of the faith community,
All: we worship God.
One: With the whole of our being,
All: let us worship God!

Opening Prayer

One: In the peace of a summer evening,
All: we know that God, our wonderful creator, is with us.
One: In the joy of a mother with her baby,
All: we are sure that God, our loving Parent, smiles on us.
One: In times of peace within the struggle,
All: we are assured that God's encouragement secures us.
One: In clear moments of hope when sickness is upon us,
All: we rejoice that it is God in whom our security rests.
One: And in this act of worship,
**All: we respond with praise to our gracious, compassionate God, and
        we give thanks for God's presence with us. Amen.**

Prayer of Reflection (Confession)

One: We hear the voice, O God, that reflects the truth about ourselves, the truth we would rather not hear.

All: **One part of us would like to silence the truth-teller;
one part of us would like to learn from that voice.**

One: We hear the voice, O God, that calls on us to revenge a wrong, real or perceived.

All: **One part of us would like to act vengefully;
one part of us would like to forgive and forget.**

One: We hear the voice, O God, that calls us to hold a grudge and not let it go.

All: **One part of us is ready to wait until we can get our own back;
one part of us would bring the grudge into the open and erase it with love.**

One: We hear the voice, O God, that recalls a promise made, which we later regret bitterly.

All: **One part of us gives the weak reminder, "You cannot go back on your word";
one part of us is ready to confess our mistake and go in a faithful direction.**

Time of reflection...

Assurance of Pardon

One: You know us so well, O God. You know the contradictions that bedevil us, the weakness we cannot counter, our unwillingness to face the dark side of our personalities.

All: **And you know that these flaws are mirrored in our community of faith.**

One: If we had to rely on ourselves we would flounder and be lost. But you, O God, will not let us go – not now, not ever.

All: **You call on us to face reality. You show us how we can replace contradictions with certainty, weakness with strength, and our dark side with the light of Christ.**

One: In Christ you will receive pardon and peace.

All: **Thanks be to God! Amen.**

Offering Prayer

One: Here we bring our gifts for your blessing, O God.
Here we bring the rewards of our labors,

All: over the past week, months, and years gone by.

One Here we dedicate our talents,

**All: to serving this faith community,
to serving our fellow men and women –
bringing reconciliation, healing, support, and caring.**

One: Here we offer our time,

**All: to bring hope in the struggle,
to enable people to fulfill their dreams,
to proclaim the forgiving way.**

One: Here we bring our gifts for your blessing, O God.

All: Amen.

Commissioning

One: Can we leave this place of worship without a prayer for peace?

**All: Can we leave this place of worship without a resolution to serve
our neighbor?**

One: Can we leave this place of worship without a commitment to our
friends in the faith community?

**All: Can we leave this place of worship without a pledge to forgive
those who have hurt us most?**

One: Can we leave this place of worship without the determination to bring
light to the dark places?

**All: Can we leave this place of worship, without heartfelt thanks to
God who has given us everything?**

Proper 11 [16]

Sunday between July 17 and July 23 inclusive

2 Samuel 7:1–14a
Psalm 89:20–37
  or Jeremiah 23:1–6 and Psalm 23
Ephesians 2:11–22
Mark 6:30–34, 53–56

Call to Worship

One: Christ is our peace;
All: we come together to praise and to pray in his name.
One: Christ is our peace;
All: we find his calm in the midst of our struggles.
One: Christ is our peace;
All: we are joined by him in a caring faith community.
One: Christ is our peace;
All: we are challenged by him to oppose fear-making forces.
One: Christ is our peace;
All: God's peace, which passes all human understanding.

Opening Prayer

One: Come with us to the place of rest and quietness, O God,
All: so that our depths of soul and spirit may know your peace.
One: Come with us to the place of reflection and prayer, O God,
All: so that we may receive the renewal that only you can give.
One: Come apart with our faith community, O God,
All: so that in the search for a fresh vision we may find the way ahead.
One: Come with us as we review our skills and talents, O God,
All: so that we may rededicate ourselves to serving those for whom Jesus cared.
Come with us and never leave us! Amen.

A Prayer for Refreshment (Confession)

One: O God, into the stress and tension of our daily lives,

All: breathe the gentle, calming influence of your Holy Spirit.

One: O God, into the fears and the doubts that disturb our faith,

All: breathe the Spirit-inspired search for truth, which casts out fear.

One: O God, into the conflicted priorities and hopes of this faith community,

All: breathe the quiet, mediating presence of your Holy Spirit.

One: O God, into the conflict ridden world where injustice is reality,

All: breathe the intent to share fairly and to resist the power hungry, through your Holy Spirit.

> *Time of reflection…*

Words of Assurance

One: Peace is your gift, O God:

All: peace of heart and of mind and of spirit.

One: Peace is your gift to the world, to the church, and to each one of us:

All: the gift of quiet acceptance, the gift of strong confrontation, the gift of simply waiting, the gift of active peacemaking, the gift of humble forgiveness, the gift of making amends.

One: Peace of heart and of mind and of spirit:

All: peace is your gift, O God. Amen.

Offering

One: The spirit in which we offer our gifts to God

All: is the spirit of thanksgiving for all God has given to us.

One: The spirit in which we offer our gifts to God

All: is the spirit of sharing from our plenty with those who need compassion and care.

One: The spirit in which we offer our gifts to God

All: is the spirit of discipleship. We rejoice in the gift of Jesus Christ and seek to follow him faithfully. Amen.

Commissioning

One: Keep us alert to your presence, O God.

All: In the early morning, may we know your Spirit with us.
In the heat of the day, in the midst of our activities, may we realize that you stay with us.
At the end of the day, as we come to rest, may we give thanks that you will never leave us.

Proper 12 [17]

Sunday between July 24 and July 30 inclusive

2 Samuel 11:1–15
Psalm 14
  or 2 Kings 4:42–44 and Psalm 145:10–18
Ephesians 3:14–21
John 6:1–21

Call to Worship

One: As we sit within this community of faith, so we are fed.

All: Praise and prayer feed our minds and spirits.

One: We are wonderfully fed.

All: The teachings of Jesus bring us to the faithful way.

One: We are graciously fed.

All: The cross of Jesus calls us to the selfless, practical way.

One: We are gloriously fed.

All: The rising of Jesus from death fills us with a timeless, unbounded hope.

Opening Prayer

One: God, you give us food and drink for each new day.

All: You are worthy of our praise!

One: God, you give us friends for the testing paths of life.

All: You are worthy of our worship!

One: God, you give us the saints as models of Christian life.

All: You are worthy of our trust!

One: God, you give us Jesus Christ to strengthen us when we take on the powers and oppressors.

All: You are worthy of our love!
Great Eternal Giver, we praise you! Amen.

A Reflection on the Weather (Confession)

One: When the sun shines brightly,

All: God encourages us to make the most of our days and to fill them with family and friends.

One: When thunder rolls across the sky and the rain pours down,

All: **God reminds us that there are storms in life, but, with faith, the good times will return.**

One: On days when the sky is black,

All: **God is there for us; God provides a glimmer of light in the darkness.**

One: When we see a rainbow in the sky,

All: **we know that God's eternal hope is there for us; our doubts and lack of confidence come to nothing.**

> *Time of reflection…*

Words of Assurance

One: O God, you are there for us on our bright and sunny days, and you are there for us when the dark, tempting forces surround us.

All: **You give us strength to come through the storm unafraid. In the turmoil and stress of new beginnings, you are there for us.**

One: We give you thanks for the reality of your peace,

All: **O forgiving God! Amen.**

Offering Prayer

One: Gifts, abundant and glorious, you shower upon us, O God, yet we often receive them without acknowledging the Gracious Giver. How can we ever thank you? Are there words enough, deeds that are good enough?

All: **We can make a start by bringing our heartfelt worship to you and by treating our fellow men and women in the way Jesus made clear. With this renewed determination, receive our gifts. Amen.**

Commissioning

One: There will be storms in life, but you will face them.

All: **The peace of God will calm us;
the courage of God will secure us;
the community of the faithful will be with us.**

One: The love of God will enfold you and never let you go!

Proper 13 [18]

Sunday between July 31 and August 6 inclusive

2 Samuel 11:26 – 12:13a
Psalm 51:1–12
    or Exodus 16:2–4, 9–15 and Psalm 78:23–29
Ephesians 4:1–16
John 6:24–35

Call to Worship

One: God, who has given us the gift of thanksgiving,
All: calls us to worship.
One: God, who has given us the gift of faithful understanding,
All: evokes joy in us as we worship.
One: God, who has given us the gift of feeling for the world's pain,
All: inspires and motivates us as we worship.
One: God, who has given us the gift of faith community,
All: gives us determination to share in the work as we worship.

Opening Prayer

One: You join us for worship, O God.
All: As we greet each other, we express your friendliness.
One: You enter into our praise, O God.
All: As we joyfully sing, we mirror your willingness to celebrate.
One: Your Word has pride of place in our reflection, O God.
All: We will take it to heart and work out its significance for our community.
One: You assure us that you will never leave us, O God.
All: We rejoice in your faithfulness in this and in every generation. Amen.

Prayer of Commitment and Confession

One: A good friend or family member is in trouble unexpectedly and we are
    called to respond promptly and sensitively.
**All: Give us the willingness to face new and unsought realities, O God,
and give us the endurance to stay beside the harshly treated ones.**

One: The community of faith has need of the skills, talent, and time that is ours.

All: **Give us the willingness to offer our best gifts to meet the challenges within the local and wider church, O God. Give us the willingness to walk in the Way of Jesus Christ.**

One: We are confronted with the need to change our way of thinking, to widen our horizons, or to recast our view of whom to support.

All: **Give us the wisdom and the courage to explore new ways and to welcome new truths.**

Time of reflection…

Words of Assurance

One: As you listen with care, reflect with openness and honesty, and act to bring change for good, you proclaim that God goes with you.

All: **God goes with us!**

One: Be assured of God's pardon and peace.

All: **Thanks be to God! Amen.**

Offering Prayer

One: Shape us, O God, as a community of grateful givers,

All: **so that as the sick know comfort,
as the downhearted gain courage,
as the troubled receive hope,
your blessing will be recognized amongst us. Amen.**

Commissioning

One: We leave this church as God's partners.

All: **Together we will face the old challenges;
together we will face the new realities;
together we will move forward without fear;
together we will bring peace and experience peace.**

One: We go out in partnership with you, O God.

Proper 14 [19]

Sunday between August 7 and August 13 inclusive

2 Samuel 18:5–9, 15, 31–33
Psalm 130
      or 1 Kings 19:4–8 and Psalm 34:1–8
Ephesians 4:25 – 5:2
John 6:35, 41–51

Call to Worship

One: Bless God at all times!

All: **We will bless and thank God at this morning service of worship.**

One: Bless God at all times!

All: **We will bless God when we celebrate birthdays and anniversaries, the markers of our human life.**

One: Bless God at all times!

All: **We will bless God when God holds us fast in the storms of life.**

One: Bless God at all times!

All: **We will bless God when we have been blessed with joy within our family or friendship circle.**

One: Bless God at all times!

All: **We will bless God when evil is confronted and the discouraged are given hope. We will bless God at all times!**

Opening Prayer

One: In the warmth of a summer evening beside the lake (in the backyard),

All: **we seek God's renewing presence.**

One: In the smile of a young mother,

All: **we seek God's parental presence.**

One: In the agony of despair, the shock of an unexpected diagnosis,

All: **we seek God's empathetic presence.**

One: In the struggles and fractures of life with family and friends,

All: **we seek God's reconciling presence. In all of life's experiences – joyful, frustrating, painful, exhilarating – and in this service of worship, Loving God, we seek your presence. Amen.**

A Prayer of Feeding (Confession)

One: You, O God, call us to look carefully at the food we receive and the food we give.

All: Is our diet and that of our family balanced in a healthy and nutritious way?

One: You, O God, call us to look carefully at our food.

All: Are we able to share from our plenty with those who live from hand to mouth?

One: You, O God, call us to look carefully at our food.

All: As we remember Christ in bread and wine, do we remember the needs of those who share the bread and wine with us?

One: You, O God, call us to look carefully at our food.

All: As we remember Jesus' words, "I am the bread of life," do we remind ourselves of our constant need for spiritual food?

Time of reflection...

Words of Assurance

One: You will nourish us, O God, if we are willing to receive the "bread of life."

All: Give us that openness to your Way, and your will, so that we will be sustained in body, mind, and spirit.

One: You will be healthy followers of Jesus Christ; the peace of Christ is yours.

All: Thanks be God! Amen.

Offering

One: In our willingness to give for the needy ones of (local area),

All: loving God, bless us.

One: In our willingness to support the hurting ones of this congregation,

All: compassionate God, bless us.

One: In our willingness to stand alongside the suffering who live far away,

All: just God, bless us, in the name of Jesus Christ. Amen.

Commissioning

One: We go from this place secure in the love of God,

All: ready to feed the hungry, ready to cheer the downhearted, ready to welcome the stranger, ready to free the imprisoned, ready to find the lost, ready to see Christ in our brothers and sisters.

One: God goes with you!

Proper 15 [20]

Sunday between August 14 and August 20 inclusive

1 Kings 2:10–12, 3:3–14
Psalm 111
>   **or Proverbs 9:1–6 and Psalm 34:9–14**
Ephesians 5:15–20
John 6:51–58

Call to Worship (Psalm 111 adapted)

One: We rejoice that we can praise you, O God, in the congregation of your people.

All: **We give you wholehearted thanks.**

One: Your covenant is secure, O God.

All: **You have stayed faithful over the generations.**

One: Your principles are right, O God.

All: **You call us to practice justice and to remain faithful.**

One: A loving respect for you, O God, is the wise course.

All: **It will lead us to praise you eternally.**

Opening Prayer (Holy Communion)

One: In bread and wine, Jesus is remembered:

All: **remembered for his teaching – simple yet profound.**

One: In bread and wine, Jesus is remembered:

All: **remembered for his community – disciples who followed and questioned.**

One: In bread and wine, Jesus is remembered:

All: **remembered for his friendship with those who were poor, despised, and rejected.**

One: In bread and wine, Jesus is remembered:

All: **remembered for his faithfulness, which led to a cross.**

One: In bread and wine, Jesus is remembered:

All: **remembered for his rising, which gives us eternal hope. For Jesus we give you thanks and praise, O God!**

Prayer of Confession

One: In our own experience, we have denied the Christ whom we follow; we ask forgiveness.

All: We have not trusted wholeheartedly, accepted readily, nor cared compassionately.

One: In our church, we have distorted the image of Christ who leads us; we ask forgiveness.

All: We have not engaged in mission enthusiastically, given talents generously, nor held a broad vision.

One: In our world, we have not acted on the message of Christ who challenges us; we ask forgiveness.

All: We have not treated the earth as sacred, its peoples with equity, nor its children as truly blessed.

Time of reflection…

Words of Assurance

One: Honest, thorough reflection comes from God;
the will to change comes from God;
and the strength for change comes from God.
Pardon is God's to grant.

All: We are God's people; we will reflect and change and receive God's pardon.

One: God's peace is yours. Believe it! Feel it!

All: Thanks be to God! Amen.

Offering Prayer (Holy Communion)

All: It is a gift that reminds us of personal nourishment, yet which speaks of spiritual nourishment.

One: O God, we give you thanks for the wine on this table.

All: It is a gift that goes beyond refreshment and speaks of love poured out.

One: O God, we give you thanks for the offering that has been taken up.

All: It is a gift that nourishes this faith community, yet which reaches out in solidarity and mutual support for all Christ's people. Amen.

Commissioning

One: Go share the Living Bread with your friends and with your enemies!

All: It is the Word that satisfies; it is the Way that leads to joy.

One: The bread is broken for the faith community.

All: The suffering will be encouraged, the lonely befriended.

One: The bread is broken for the world.

All: The refugee will be accepted, the oppressed set free.

One: The bread is broken for each one of you.

All: For our personal challenge, for our spiritual nourishment.

One: The Living Bread:

All: Jesus Christ, the Living Bread!

Proper 16 [21]

Sunday between August 21 and August 27 inclusive

1 Kings 8:(1, 6, 10–11), 22–30, 41–43
Psalm 84
>   **or Joshua 24:1–2a, 14–18 and Psalm 34:15–22**
Ephesians 6:10–20
John 6:56–69

Call to Worship

One: Follow God's signs to the place of worship and open your hearts with praise and thanksgiving. The beauty of flowers, the chorus of birdsong, the glimmer of sunrise,

All: **invite us to worship God, creator and sustainer of life.**

One: The smiles and laughter of children at play (running through the sprinkler),

All: **invite us to worship God, who wishes us to enjoy life to the full.**

One: The struggle of persons who are sick or enduring life's trials,

All: **invite us to worship God, whose way is compassion and wholeness.**

One: The crying needs of our well-populated planet,

All: **invite us to worship God, the source of justice and mercy for all people.**

Opening Prayer

One: You have walked with us, O God, in the joys and challenges of daily life.

All: **You will walk with us now.**

One: You have been our companion in the families and the faith communities of which we are a part.

All: **You will accompany us in the coming days.**

One: You have gone with us into the heartache of this small corner of the world.

All: **You will never leave us.**

One: You have been an instrument for peace and compassion in the past and you will renew your dedication as we worship this morning.

All: **In all the changes of life, you were there, you are there, and you will be there. Thanks be to you, O God! Amen.**

Prayer of Confidence/Confession (based on Ephesians 6:10–17)

One: Equip us, O God, to be your people. We need the whole range of Christian values and talents, if we are to withstand the dark forces and the self-serving choices of this world.

All: **Enable us to speak the truth, even when this costs us dearly.**

One: The truth will make you free!

All: **Give us the strength to follow the right way, the path of clear conscience.**

One: The righteous path is not an easy one!

All: **Help us make the gospel of peace relevant to our friends.**

One: The life, death, and rising of Jesus is still the best of all good news!

All: **Strengthen our faith so that it will hold us strong when temptation comes.**

One: May your faith be a rock in your hour of need!

All: **Although we do not have all the spiritual equipment we need, with God's Spirit and God's Word, we will know and share God's saving grace.**

One: God will be your companion and guide!

Time of reflection…

Words of Assurance

One: When it seems that being a contemporary follower of Jesus Christ is beyond us, God breaks through and gives us a sign of hope.

All: **A child is noticed for giving an honest response, a friend hears an encouraging word from the scriptures, a sufferer takes heart in the midst of crisis. We know we are not alone!**

One: God will never give up on you or desert you; God is with you for the long haul!

All: **Thanks be to God! Amen.**

Offering Prayer

One: May your blessing, O God, bring these gifts to life:

All: **fresh ways of coping,**
a chance to work, a chance to rest,
a way to live gracefully, a way to die peacefully.

One: May these gifts be used as Jesus Christ would use them. Amen.

Commissioning

One: We dedicate ourselves to you, O God.

All: **We will be faithful in following Jesus;**
we will be joyful as we go about our week;
we will be ready to help the disadvantaged;
we will play an active part in the faith community;
we will be conscious of the terrorized and changing world;
we will never rest until all have been challenged by the teaching,
death, and rising of Jesus Christ.

Proper 17 [22]

Sunday between August 28 and September 3 inclusive

Song of Solomon 2:8–13
Psalm 45:1–2, 6–9
    or Deuteronomy 4:1–2, 6–9 and Psalm 15
James 1:17–27
Mark 7:1–8, 14–15, 21–23

Call to Worship

One: Ever-present God, you are with us at this time of worship.

All: **In our praise, you are the note of joy;**
        in our praying, you are the still small voice;
        in our listening, you are the word that hits home;
        in our fellowship, you are the friendly hand held out;
        in our call to serve, you are the source of inspiration.

One: With confidence and trust,

All: **We will worship God!**

Opening Prayer

One: God of all of life's seasons, you are with us.

All: **In the glory days of summer and in the frigid depths of winter, you**
        are with us.

One: You are with us, God.

All: **In the enthusiasm of youth and in the reflective advancing years,**
        you are with us.

One: You are with us, God.

All: **In the rushed days of productive work and in the slower pace of**
        retirement, you are with us.

One: You are with us, God.

All: **In the dark night of the soul and in the morning when joy over-**
        flows, you are with us.

One: You never leave us, God.

All: **You will never leave us, in time or beyond time. Amen.**

Prayer of Confession

One: You remind us, O God, that people are not always what they appear to be.

All: On the outside they appear to be friendly and accommodating, but on the inside they are wary and suspicious. And we are sometimes like that.

One: You caution us, O God, that people are not always what they appear to be.

All: On the outside they seem knowledgeable and wise, but this is a front for uncertainty and biased opinions. And we are sometimes like that.

One: You warn us, O God, that people are not always what they appear to be.

All: On the outside they seek the opportunity to work with others, but this masks an ambition to get their own way. And we are sometimes like that.

One: You put us on our guard, O God; people are not always what they appear to be.

All: On the outside they follow Jesus, your Chosen One, but their faith denies justice for the poor and despised ones. And we are sometimes like that.

> *Time of reflection...*

Words of Assurance

One: You are not fooled, O God. You see us as we really are and you stand ready to change us for good.

All: Where we hold back from the truth, you call us to account.
Where we lack the courage to confront, you empower us.
Where we will not apologize, you enable us.
Where our words are not matched by deeds, you inspire us.
Where our discipleship is lackluster, you enthuse us.

One: When change becomes reality, peace follows and pardon is experienced.

All: And we are renewed. Thanks be to God! Amen.

Offering Prayer

One: These are good gifts, O God.

All: **May they restore the downhearted,**
encourage those without hope,
bring wholeness to the sick,
put zest back into lives that lack interest and direction,
and go to work in communities far from the shores of this nation.

One: Bless these gifts, O God, as they bring change in the Way of Jesus Christ. Amen.

Commissioning

One: You are sent out to be Christians of integrity:

All: **to search for the truth with courage and tenacity,**
to counter the powerful with persistence and honesty,
to work against evil with single-mindedness and determination,
to listen to the opinions of others with patience and with an
open mind,
to work with others with dedication and good humor,
to follow Jesus Christ with faithfulness and enthusiasm.

One: The One God, wise, fearless, all-knowing, embraces you with love!

Proper 18 [23]

Sunday between September 4 and September 10 inclusive

Proverbs 22:1–2, 8–9, 22–23
Psalm 125
　　or Isaiah 35:4–7a and Psalm 146
James 2:1–10, (11–13), 14–17
Mark 7:24–37

Call to Worship

One: This is a place of thanksgiving.
All: We rejoice that we are here.
One: This is a time to bring praise and prayer to God.
All: We rejoice in the opportunity for worship.
One: These are the friends who have become our church family.
All: We rejoice that they are persons to trust and support.
One: This is the Christ who goes ahead to challenge us.
All: We rejoice that Christ's inspiration has been there for us and always will be.
Let us worship God!

Opening Prayer

One: Creator God, we praise you!
All: The beauty of the sunset, the colors of hill and harvest leave us breathless with praise.
One: Holy God, we adore you!
All: The wonder, mystery, and peace of your presence leave us in awe.
One: God, Our Friend, we worship you!
All: You are known to us in times of deepest joy and in times of hard testing.
One: Just and loving God, we listen to you!
All: We will work your purpose out when evil threatens and fear looms large.
One: God revealed in Jesus, we pledge our discipleship!
All: We will bring the peace of Christ to those who suffer and the compassion of Christ to those who need support. Amen.

A Prayer of Faith and Confession (Option 1, Mark 7:24–37)

One: In the name of Jesus Christ, we have created community in this place.

All: **Forgive us, God, when our faith community lacks vision or enthusiasm.**

One: In the name of Jesus Christ, we have made the cross a symbol of healing.

All: **Forgive us, God, when we ignore the crying needs of those we don't know, those whose distress does not touch us.**

One: In the name of Jesus Christ, we have proclaimed that the truth will make us free.

All: **Forgive us, God, when we close our minds to new ways of thinking, fresh sources of inspiration.**

One: In the name of Jesus Christ, we believe that forgiveness may be received.

All: **Forgive us, God, when we will not let our guilt go, when we claim your love cannot reach us.**

  Time of reflection…

Words of Assurance

One: Your assurance is ours, O God.

All: **Nothing is beyond your power to enlighten, to heal, and to forgive. Eternal source of hope, we rejoice that new beginnings open up for us.**

One: Pardon and peace are yours to accept.

All: **We will know peace, thanks be to God! Amen.**

Prayer of Confession (Option 2, Proverbs 22:1–2 ff)

One: Loving God, how easy it is to give a person a bad name:

All: **to pass along rumors and stories,**
  to stress the dark side rather than the light side,
  to transfer our own faults to others,
  to make assumptions and ignore the facts,
  to judge on a troubled past,
  to apply community values that are self-serving and materialistic.
  Time of reflection…

Assurance of Pardon

One: In refusing to judge, in seeking the best in another, in putting the past in the past;

in affirming the work and worth of another in God's sight,

All: we bring honor to the Name that is above every other name.

One: Pardon and peace are yours!

All: Thanks be to God! Amen.

Offering Prayer

One: You have gifted each one of us, living God:

All: some with spontaneous friendship,

some with the ability to plan,

some with an observant eye,

some with a generous nature,

some with warm compassion.

One: Bless our gifts of personality.

All: Bless all our gifts, so that the Way of Jesus may be advanced in this faith community and throughout the world. Amen.

Commissioning

One: Go forth in the strong name of Jesus Christ!

All: We will feed the hungry;

we will comfort the sick and those who mourn;

we will stir up the apathetic;

we will encourage the timid;

we will challenge the complacent;

we will confront the dark powers;

we will be ready for sacrifice.

One: The spirit of Jesus is yours!

Proper 19 [24]

Sunday between September 11 and September 17 inclusive

Proverbs 1:20–33
Psalm 19
    or Isaiah 50:4–9a and Psalm116:1–9
James 3:1–12
Mark 8:27–38

Call to Worship

One: We gather to worship:

All: **a sign that we are faithful to God.**

One: We greet each other with "The Peace":

All: **a sign that we trust and support each other in the faith community.**
(Pass the peace, in whatever way is appropriate in your tradition.)

One: We listen for God's word to us:

All: **a sign that God, who has spoken in times past, still speaks to the people of God.**

One: We resolve to serve the living God:

All: **a sign that our faith has meaning and purpose for good, meaning and purpose for ourselves, and meaning and purpose for those in our community who have practical and spiritual needs.**

Opening Prayer

One: At the dawn of a new day, you are with us, O God,

All: **filling us with hope, giving us a clear vision of the way to be taken.**

One: In the heat of the day, you are with us, O God,

All: **strengthening us in the struggle and encouraging us when the way ahead is rough and testing.**

One: In the cool of the evening, you are with us, O God,

All: **calling us to thanksgiving, enabling us to reflect on our experiences along the way.**

One: In this service, you are with us, O God,

All: **calling us to follow Jesus, who is the way, the truth, and the life. Amen.**

Prayer of Confession

One: Rejection is difficult to endure, O God – rejection by our family, by our friends, or by faith community members.

All: **We will affirm our chosen goals, our proven abilities, our right to walk the path of faithfulness.**

One: "Carrying the cross," is a challenging process, O God. It calls for Christian commitment beyond our accepted limits.

All: **We will face the daily tests, the temptation to practice self-serving ways and to ignore community, the temptation to compromise with the evil ones. We will walk the path of discipleship.**

One: Keeping true to gospel values is no easy task, O God – being honest, showing compassion, confronting the powerful, accepting the despised.

All: **We will find strength in the spirit and example of Jesus Christ. We will walk his Way with determination.**

> *Time of reflection...*

omit

Words of Assurance

One: You build us up, O God. You give us confidence; you sustain us.

All: **In our times of uncertainty, you are the secure One.**
In our times of weakness, you strengthen us.
In our lonely times, your friendship is there for us.
You allow us to doubt and to question, and when fear takes hold of us, your love will not let us go.

One: You, O God, stand ready to give us a fresh start.

All: **Pardon and peace are ours. Thanks be to God! Amen.**

Offering Prayer

One: It is through your goodness, most graceful God, that we have become a gifted people.

All: **Open us to the joy of sharing our gifts with others so that with money offered, time usefully spent, and our natural talents generously used, your work may be done and your name glorified. Amen.**

Commissioning

One: On the road that led to the cross, God stayed with Jesus, and, in our testing times, God will stay with us too.

All: **The source of hope, when we are discouraged;**
the source of community, when we are on our own;
the source of faith, when doubt overpowers us;
the source of inspiration, when life is colorless and drab;
the source of eternity, when the weight of years bears down on us;
the source of peace, when uncertainty is all around us...

One: God will not leave you on your own!

All: **Praise be to God!**

Proper 20 [25]

Sunday between September 18 and September 24 inclusive

Proverbs 31:10–31
Psalm 1
> or Wisdom of Solomon 1:16 – 2:1, 12-22 or Jeremiah 11:18–20
> Psalm 54
James 3:13 – 4:3, 7–8a
Mark 9:30–37

Call to Worship

One: The casual, thoughtful word of a good friend
All: can open up a way for us to encourage or to forgive.
One: The simple, generous act of a caring neighbor
All: can bring home to us the esteem in which we are held.
One: The carefully phrased note from a family member
All: can be the symbol of a love deep and profound.
One: And this time of worship – familiar, routine, imperfect –
All: can be a faithful reminder of God's wonderful love for us.

Opening Prayer

One: The hug of a family member joyfully reunited
All: makes clear your wholehearted love for us, O God.
One: The singer bursting forth into glorious song
All: encourages us to praise and thank you without limit, O God.
One: The reader caught up in the pages of a great novel
**All: inspires us to watch for your word in scripture and to find the
message for us.**
One: The researcher carefully exploring new territory
**All: prompts us to look for fresh spiritual truth, unafraid of what
might be revealed.**
One: Jesus Christ, full of compassion; with clear intuition; honoring God's
word; fearless, forgiving:
All: Jesus is our pattern as we worship. Amen.

Prayer of Confession

One: "Then he took a child and put it among them."

All: **When we use long words and confusing sentences, put a child among us.**

One: When we let the cares of the world drag us down, when the demands of life seem overwhelming, put a child among us.

All: **When we are tempted to deceive or to selfishly sway an opinion, put a child among us.**

One: When we need love, recognition, or a great big hug, put a child

All: amily, or community in

Welcome and Call to Worship
We are here to praise you, lift our hearts and sing

Wor
One
All:

The thoughtful word of a good friend
can open up a new spirit in our hearts
The generous act of a caring neighbour them."
can raise our self esteem
The quick note from a family member lenges our attitudes and
can be a symbol of deep love

One
And this time we share together
can remind us of God's blessings to us
All:
Let us worship God and sing together..

Offering Prayer

One: As you increase our wisdom, loving God, so you increase our vision of need.

All: **We see the loneliness of some congregational members;**
we hear the call of youngsters for a safe and fun place to hang out;
we respond to the appeal of those who are sick or housebound for someone to listen to them;
we recognize the desperation of refugees and the plight of the homeless.

One: Your gifts will be blessed by God, as they go to work to bring change.

All: **Praise be to God! Amen.**

Commissioning

One: Give us, O God, a childlike simplicity as we leave this faith community:

All: **joy, in the unforeseen opportunities and blessings;**
simplicity, as we respond to need and cries for help;
care, for the sad and afraid;
wonder, in the face of nature's beauty;
and peace, as we feel your love around us, O most loving God.

Proper 21 [26]

Sunday between September 18 and September 24 inclusive

Esther 7:1–6, 9–10, 9:20–22
Psalm 124
      or Numbers 11:4–6, 10–16, 24–29 and Psalm 19:7–14
James 5:13–20
Mark 9:38–50

Call to Worship

One: You call us to worship, O God; you call us to prayer.
All: **As we express our thanks, as we pray for the troubled, as we confess our shortcomings, you hear us.**
One: You call us to worship, O God; you inspire us to praise.
All: **As we sing the hymns, as we respond in the psalms, you join with us.**
One: You call us worship, O God; you call us to hear the Word.
All: **As we listen to the scriptures, as we are touched by the Word proclaimed, you speak to us.**
One: You call us to worship, O God; you call us to the Communion table.
All: **As we eat the bread, as we drink the wine, as we remember Jesus Christ, your love unites us.**

Opening Prayer

One: If God is with us,
All: **we will be able to bring our thanksgivings to church, but also our worries.**
One: If God is with us,
All: **we will be able to enjoy the laughter of children, but also hear the concerns of older folk.**
One: If God is with us,
All: **we will be able to consider the needs of this faith community, but also the needs of the oppressed far from here.**
One: If God is with us,
All: **the impact of Jesus' teaching will come home to us, but his cross-death will face us with new realities.**

One: *If* God is with us?
All: **God is with us! Amen.**

A Prayer of Aspiration (Confession)

One: What is gained for God is worth the sacrifice.
All: **Acts of compassion and deeds of caring are worth the time taken from free-time and leisure.**
One: What is gained for God is worth the sacrifice.
All: **Words that speak of justice, letters that call for freedom are worth the opposition and the anger aroused.**
One: What is gained for God is worth the sacrifice.
All: **Work as a part of the faith community; teamwork to help the young, the challenged, and the infirm is worth more than going it alone.**
One: What is gained for God is worth the sacrifice.
All: **Following the Way of Christ, giving priority to prayer and praise is worth the ridicule, is worth comparison with the world's values.**
      Time of reflection...

Words of Assurance

One: We follow Jesus Christ, who sacrificed his life so that evil would be exposed and God's love would triumph.
All: **The testing of Jesus, the fickleness of his friends, and his death on the cross reveal the small scale of our sacrifice.**
One: Are you ready to renew your faithfulness? Are you ready to walk the tough and costly path?
All: **We are ready!**
One: Peace is yours. Find joy in a fresh start.
All: **Thanks be to God! Amen.**

Offering Prayer

One: You have gifted us, O God, with wisdom, compassion, and the ability to love. Bless these gifts, that through them

All: **those who are perplexed may find wisdom,**
those who are distressed may find compassion,
and those who are rejected may find love.

One: We pray in the name of Jesus the Giver.

All: **Amen.**

Commissioning

One: The God who called you to this place of worship sends you out to proclaim the Good News to your small corner of the world.

All: **We will go in hope, for God goes before us.**
We will go in joy, for God is our companion.
We will go with courage, for God believes in us.
We will go in peace, for God's peace will keep us eternally secure.

One: In God's presence and knowing Christ's love, you have nothing to fear and life eternal to gain!

Proper 22 [27]

Sunday between October 2 and October 8 inclusive

Job 1:1, 2:1–10
Psalm 26
    or Genesis 2:18–24 and Psalm 8
Hebrews 1:1–4, 2:5–12
Mark 10:2–16

Call to Worship

One: In our singing,
All: **O God, be the note of joy.**
One: In our praying,
All: **O God, be the heartfelt word.**
One: In our searching,
All: **O God, be the will to endure.**
One: In our need,
All: **O God, be the source of hope.**
One: In our serving,
All: **O God, be the hands and feet of Christ.**

Opening Prayer

One: God spoke through creation and the wonders of nature
All: **and we are challenged to respond with care and with responsibility.**
One: God spoke through prophets and wise leaders
All: **and we are called to respond by seeking justice and by practicing kindness.**
One: God spoke through the teachings, the cross-death, and the rising of Jesus,
All: **and we are called to respond by following faithfully and by serving wholeheartedly.**
One: God still speaks through prayer and through humble saints
All: **and we are called to respond in our worship, in our care for one another, and in our concern for the poor and powerless.**
One: Listen for the voice of God!
All: **It is the voice we long to hear. Amen.**

Prayer of Confession

One: You know our place of testing, O God.

All: **We are tested in the relationships of marriage and family, tested in the ties of friendship and companionship. Will we remain faithful?**

One: You are with us in the place of testing, O God.

All: **We are tested in the use of our talents and abilities, tested in our choice of priorities. Will we remain faithful?**

One: You stay with us at the time of testing, O God.

All: **We are tested by the forces of power and darkness, tested to compromise and encouraged to look the other way. Will we remain faithful?**

One: You will not forsake us when our community is tested, O God,

All: **tested by change and unforeseen opportunity, tested by newcomers and fresh patterns of service. Will we remain faithful?**

Time of reflection…

Words of Assurance

One: You understand us so well, O God. You understand our good intentions; you understand how we rationalize and go astray.

All: **But you will renew our faithfulness, restore the strength of our discipleship, and bring us back to the Way of Jesus Christ again.**

One: The failures of the past will be left in the past; a new day has dawned. Pardon and peace are reality.

All: **God be praised! Amen.**

Offering Prayer

One: As we present our gifts, O God,

All: **open our eyes to everything you have gifted to us.**

One: As we share, O God,

All: **open our hearts to the sick, the troubled, and the bereaved.**

One: As we have been richly blessed, O God,

All: **open our minds to the way in which we can be a blessing to others, as Jesus was a blessing to us. Amen.**

Commissioning

One: You grant us a new Way, O God:

All: **understanding in our crucial relationships,**
endurance in the time of testing,
peace when the storm breaks over us,
faith when doubt threaten us,
community when loneliness confronts us,
and your love within us, before us, and behind us –
a sustained, trustworthy love.

One: On God you can rely.

Proper 23 [28]

Sunday between October 9 and October 15 inclusive

Job 23:1–9, 16–17
Psalm 22:1–15
  or Amos 5:6–7, 10–15 and Psalm 90:12–17
Hebrews 4:12–16
Mark 10:17–31

Call to Worship

One: You will prosper our worship, O God.

All: **Every hymn, every prayer, every word of the Word will count, if you are with us.**

One: You will prosper our witness, O God.

All: **Every friend cared for, every family member listened to, every faithful contact made will count, if you are with us.**

One: You will prosper our service, O God.

All: **Every powerless one encouraged, every downhearted person given hope, every dark deed exposed will count, if you are with us.**

Opening Prayer

One: Your love, O God, will not let us go!

All: **As we stand in awe of creation, your love is "wonder-ful."**

One: Your love, O God, will not let us go!

All: **As we struggle to let go the past, your love is forgiving.**

One: Your love, O God, will not let us go!

All: **As we strengthen this faith community, your love binds us together.**

One: Your love, O God, will not let us go!

All: **As we serve as disciples, your love comes clear in the life of Jesus. Amen.**

Prayer of Confession

One: As persons who share your wonderful creation, we are rich indeed, O God.

All: **The crisp snow of winter, the budding of spring, the fruits of the harvest, the hues of fall, proclaim our plenty. When we take your bounty for granted, forgive us!**

One: As persons who share in community, we are rich indeed, O God.

All: **The joy within family, the trust of friendship, the support of our neighbors, proclaim our plenty. When we seek our own good first, forgive us!**

One: As persons who share in the family of faith, we are rich indeed, O God.

All: **The opportunities for worship, the encouragement given and received, the challenge to care and serve, proclaim our plenty. When we will not share in faith community, forgive us!**

One: As persons who share in the discipleship of Jesus Christ, we are rich indeed, O God.

All: **His inspiring teachings, his opposition to evil, his willingness to sacrifice, his glorious rising, proclaim our plenty. When we fail in faithfulness, forgive us!**

Time of reflection…

Words of Assurance

One: Great giving God, we praise you! You know well the poverty of our response to all you have given us.

All: **We have taken your goodness for granted; we have failed to measure up to your trust; we have squandered our rich inheritance; and we are sorry.**

One: God knows the extent of your failure; God hears your sincere confession; God believes you are ready to make a fresh start; God grants the pardon and peace of new beginnings.

All: **Thanks be to God! Amen.**

Offering Prayer

One: If we could grasp God's rich provision for us,

All: we would give generously.

One: If we could enter into the relief and celebration of those who share our gifts,

All: our joy would know no bounds.

One: If we could add to these gifts the gifts of skill, understanding, and compassion,

All: we would experience a full sense of God's blessing. May it be so! Amen.

Commissioning

One: Let us go from here as those who know true wealth:

**All: the sound of a waterfall,
the beauty of a sunset,
the joy of children's laughter,
the embrace of a loved one,
the trust of a friend,
a good bed at the end of the day,
a favorite hymn sung in our own church,
the companionship of serving the needy,
the life, death, and rising of Jesus Christ.**

One: You are wealthy indeed!

Proper 24 [29]

Sunday between October 16 and October 22 inclusive

Job 38:1–7, (34–41)
Psalm 104:1–9, 24, 35c
    or Isaiah 53:4–12 and Psalm 91:9–16
Hebrews 5:1–10
Mark 10:35–45

Call to Worship

One: Greet this morning with joy!

All: **A new week with all its opportunities lies ahead of us.**

One: Greet this morning with thanksgiving!

All: **This is the time of praise and prayer, the time to remember God's creative generosity.**

One: Greet this morning with care!

All: **We are aware of our responsibility as people of God.**

One: Greet this morning with Christ!

All: **On the first day of the week we celebrate Christ's rising from death.**

Opening Prayer

One: If only humankind would face the consequences of its actions,

All: **your realm of justice and peace, O God, would be clearer and come closer.**

One: If only humankind would realize the Source of its life-giving goodness,

All: **worship would be inspired and faith communities would throb with new life.**

One: If only the church would sense its need to venture into a suffering world,

All: **mission would be alive again and persons would take to heart the compassionate example of Jesus Christ.**

One: If only the impact of Jesus could be felt in our personal lives,

All: **each moment would be fully lived and our struggles would be endured faithfully.**

One: O God, bring our most cherished hopes to reality!

All: **Amen.**

The Cost of Discipleship (A Confessional Prayer)

One: There is a cost to our discipleship and this we acknowledge before you, O God.

All: There are times when we cannot reconcile the needs of our family with our life of faith.

One: There is a cost to our discipleship and we lay it before you, O God.

All: There are times when the way we are called to work conflicts with the ethical Christian way.

One: There is a cost to our discipleship and we bring it to you, O God.

All: There are times when our commitment to the community of faith takes second place to our own needs and desires.

One: There is a cost to our discipleship and we confess it to you, O God.

All: There are times when the broad vision of Christian concern and action gets lost among trivial local issues.

One: Jesus asked, "Are you able to drink the cup that I drink, or be baptized with the baptism that I am baptized with?"

All: We will think carefully and prayerfully about our response.
Time of reflection...

Words of Assurance

One: The willingness of Jesus to face the cost of faithfulness, and to go to the cross, stops us in our tracks. It causes us to rethink our life's journey.

All: The change in perspective affects every area of our life; it colors our choices and decisions.

One: It is tough to disturb relationships, stressful to make a change in direction, but doing so will bring you God's all-embracing peace.

All: In God's strength we are ready.

One: God will be your companion.

All: Thanks be to God! Amen.

Offering Prayer

One: We offer these gifts for renewal through the faith community, O God.

All: **Through these gifts, may the lonely find friendship;**
through these gifts, may the sick find hope;
through these gifts, may those who suffer find comfort;
through these gifts, may the powerless gain confidence;
through these gifts, may the Way of Jesus Christ be experienced.

One: Bless us the givers, and bless those who receive these gifts.

All: **Amen.**

Commissioning

One: What will change as a result of our morning's act of worship?

All: **Will we realize our responsibilities as Christians in a**
materialistic world?
Will we be aware of our need for wholeness and healing?
Will we find ways to encourage the downhearted?
Will we understand that true greatness lies in humility?
Will we take a significant place in the life of the faith community?
Will we recognize the cost of discipleship?
Will we be able to follow the sacrificial Way of Jesus Christ?

One: There will be changes; your faithfulness will be restored.

Proper 25 [30]

Sunday between October 23 and October 29 inclusive

Job 42:1–6, 10–17
Psalm 34:1–8, (19–22)
    or Jeremiah 31:7–9 and Psalm 126
Hebrews 7:23–28
Mark 10:46–52

Call to Worship

One: God, creator of the universe, creator of planet Earth,

All: we adore you in our worship!

One: God, inspiration of our faith community,

All: we praise you in our worship!

One: God, who opens our eyes to the needs of faith communities throughout the world,

All: we are challenged to share through our worship!

One: God, whose compassionate and merciful way is known in Jesus Christ,

All: we respond with our love to his love. Let us worship God!

Opening Prayer

One: We glory in your creative miracle, O God.

**All: Your world is so wonderful: the sunrise, the vast seas, the mountain
ranges, and the gift of life to each one of us.**

One: We glory in your sustaining miracle, O God:

**All: the certainty of the returning seasons, the growing awareness of
young children.**

One: We glory in your miraculous Word, O God,

**All: which reveals your loving presence and which challenges us to
bring hope.**

One: We glory in Jesus, the miracle of New Life,

**All: who enabled the blind to see, the disciples to have insight, and the
despised to know power. God of miracles, we joyfully adore you!
Amen.**

Prayer of Confession

One: Open our eyes, O God!

All: **Enable us to see the cost of injustice, as well as the fruits of prosperity.**

One: Open our eyes, O God!

All: **Enable us to see the hopes and dreams of loved ones, as well as our own defined goals.**

One: Open our eyes, O God!

All: **Enable us to see our own faults, as clearly as the faults of others.**

One: Open our eyes, O God!

All: **Enable us to see how our faith community can meet neighborhood needs and serve the global church.**

One: Open our eyes, O God!

All: **For your way of seeing, revealed in Jesus, lights our way with truth and calls us to action.**

> *Time of reflection…*

Assurance of Pardon

One: You will open our eyes, O God,

All: **with a fresh vision of ourselves and of how we relate to others,**

One: with a renewed way of seeing our church and its place in the family of faith communities,

All: **with a realistic sense of our world and of our part in changing it for good.**

One: With eyes open to the truth,
with minds resolved to bring change,
with hearts afire with the zeal of Jesus Christ,
you will make a new start.

All: **Pardon and peace will be ours! Amen.**

Offering Prayer

One: Rejoice and be thankful!
Rejoice and give generously!
Rejoice and share wholeheartedly!
Rejoice and praise God continually!

All: This faith community will rejoice with us,
faith communities in this country will rejoice with us,
faith communities in every part of the world will rejoice with us,
for this offering will be a blessing, and we will receive a blessing.
Amen.

Commissioning

One: Open your eyes; rejoice in the glory of God's creation!
Open your eyes; rejoice in the friendships you have made and can make!
Open your eyes; rejoice in the church family who supports you and
who is with you!
Open your eyes; rejoice in the challenges of the week that lies ahead
of you!
Open your heart; rejoice in the God who goes with you and who will
sustain you!

All: **We are wide eyed, waiting in joy and in hope!**

Proper 26 [31]

Sunday between October 30 and November 5 inclusive

Ruth 1:1–18
Psalm 146
  or Deuteronomy 6:1–9 and Psalm 119:1–8
Hebrews 9:11–14
Mark 12:38–44

Call to Worship (from Psalm 146)

One: Praise the Lord!

All: We will praise God as long as we live.

One: Happy are those whose faith is in God!

All: God keeps faith forever.

One: God's justice is for the oppressed!

All: Food for the hungry, freedom for the prisoners, sight for the blind.

One: The Lord watches over strangers

All: and supports the orphan and the widow.

One: The Lord will reign forever!

All: Yes! We will praise God!

Opening Prayer

One: Proclaim confidently that God reigns.

All: We rejoice that God has never left us and never will leave us.

One: Make clear the relevance of God's Word.

All: We rejoice that the challenge of the prophets and the teaching of Jesus is for us and always will be for us.

One: Be sure all are within God's care.

All: The helpless baby, the active teenager, the busy young mother, the volunteering senior: none are separated from God's love.

One: Bring praise and thanks to God, for all God is and all God will be.

All: We sing with our voices, we respond with our mind, we return love from the depth of our hearts. Amen.

Prayer of Confession (Mark 12:29–31)

One: "Listen carefully; God is One."

All: **We have served other gods: the god of money, the god of self-interest, the god of work.**

One: "Love your God with all your heart, and with all your soul, and with all your mind, and with all your strength."

All: **We have forgotten God in the rush of the day, in unforeseen worries, in the demands of family.**

One: "...and love your neighbor as yourself..."

All: **We have neglected our neighbor; we have not said the caring word, not had the time to listen, not been ready to forgive.**

One: "....and love your neighbor as *yourself*."

All: **We have neglected ourselves; we have failed to celebrate our gifts, have made light of praise, and have not taken time out to "smell the roses."**

> *Time of reflection...*

Words of Assurance

One: If you love God, then everything falls into place.

All: **Worship and helping our neighbor become priorities and come naturally; we free up time to attend to our own needs.**

One: God's peace is yours!

All: **Thanks be to God. Amen.**

Offering Prayer

One: It is in our offering, O God, that our faithfulness to you is proved.

All: **You call us to build up this faith community.**
You call us to encourage each other.
You call us to serve the sick and the dying.
You call us to widen our ideas of church.
You call us to serve the dispossessed.

One: As you give generously, as you give appropriately, so you are blessed.

All: **Praise God! Amen.**

Commissioning

One: Love with a love that defies fear.

All: We will love with a love that will not give in.

One: Love with a love that seeks the best.

All: We will love with a love that will not see the worst.

One: Love with a love that finds joy in community.

All: We will love with a love that makes friends.

One: Love with a love that crosses boundaries.

All: We will love with a love that confronts evil, wherever it is found.

Proper 27 [32]

Sunday between November 6 and November 12 inclusive

Ruth 3:1–5, 4:13–17
Psalm 127
> or 1 Kings 17:8–16 and Psalm 146

Hebrews 9:24–28
Mark 12:38–44

Call to Worship

One: You notice when we come to worship, O God.

All: **Your heart is warmed by our praise.**

One: You notice when we respond to your word, O God.

All: **Your heart is warmed when we go your way.**

One: You notice when *we* notice the downtrodden.

All: **Your heart is warmed when we work with them for change.**

One: You notice each one of us and know us by name.

All: **Your heart is warmed when we bring glory to your name.**

Opening Prayer

One: The simple words of children, O God,

All: **are good enough to offer prayers to you.**

One: The straightforward melody of an ancient hymn, O God,

All: **is good enough to sing praise to you.**

One: The kindly deed of a neighbor, O God,

All: **is enough to make clear Christ's presence.**

One: The sacrifice of one person for another, O God,

All: **is enough to show that your love will never die. Amen.**

Prayer of Confession

One: Grant us the gift of humility, O God.

All: **When we catch ourselves showing off, humble us!**

One: Grant us the gift of humility, O God.

All: **When we insist on our own way, transform us!**

One: Grant us the gift of humility, O God.

All: **When we downplay the gifts of others, correct us!**

One: Grant us the gift of humility, O God.

All: When we have inflated expectations, deflate us!

One: Grant us the gift of humility, O God,

All: and in talking less and serving more, in boasting less and praying more, humble us!

Time of reflection...

Words of Assurance

One: As you work quietly yet effectively, as you follow the Way of Christ and the serving saints, you will know the peace God reserves for the humble.

All: We will rejoice, for God's pardon will be ours. Thanks be to God! Amen.

Offering Prayer

One: If only you could see where your gifts make their mark:

All: where the distressed are counseled,
among the downhearted and the depressed,
among the working poor,
on hospital wards,
in apartments nobody notices,
in minefield-infested areas,
among the oppressed and the refugee,

One: then your generosity would overflow and God would smile.

All: Amen.

Commissioning

One: With God's help, you will make a difference!

All: We will recognize the tested.
We will notice the suffering.
We will support the dispirited.
We will motivate the apathetic.
We will inspire the faithless.
We will serve the poorest.
We will get involved in the movement for justice.

One: God will be at your side!

Proper 28 [33]

Sunday between November 13 and November 19 inclusive

1 Samuel 1:4–20
1 Samuel 2:1–10
      or Daniel 12:1–3 and Psalm 16
Hebrews 10:11–14, (15–18), 19–25
Mark 13:1–8

Call to Worship

One: Times are changing.

All: In the midst of change, you are the rock, O God, the place of security.

One: Times are changing.

All: In the midst of change, you are the strong one, O God, the source of courage.

One: Times are changing.

All: In the midst of change, you are the One longed for, O God, the root of peace.

Opening Prayer (Hannah's Prayer, 1 Samuel 2:1–10 adapted)

(God has answered Hannah's prayer for a child and she gives thanks to God.)

One: God has filled my heart with joy;

All: we are happy at all God has done.

One: God's love goes beyond imagining;

All: God's greatness is beyond understanding.

One: God restores life and hope;

All: God gives a sense of self-worth to the poor and provides community to the lonely.

One: God stands in solidarity with the faithful

All: and works to bring light to the world's dark places.

One: In the coming days, God's purposes will be fulfilled;

All: the kingdom of God's Chosen One will triumph! Amen.

Prayer of Longing (Confession)

One: We long for security amid a changing world:

All: **the terrorists strike, the towers fall, the civilized order is threatened.**

One: We long for security, in a changing family situation:

All: **the ties of marriage are strained, addictions are acquired early, debt is easy to come by.**

One: We long for security in a changing church:

All: **the old tunes and traditions are replaced, patterns of worship are new, there is a different level of commitment.**

One: We long for security, in a changing faith:

All: **questioning and doubt are front and center, the person of Jesus is debated, the scriptures are probed.**

   Time of reflection...

Words of Assurance

One: Does God change?

All: **God is the wonderful constant in a changing world.**

One: Does the message of Jesus Christ change?

All: **"Love God, and love your neighbor as you love yourself," is as valid now as it was 2000 years ago.**

One: Is the Holy Spirit still at work?

All: **Friends still encourage, the downhearted are still lifted up, and the wicked and the powerful are still opposed.**

One: You have your security!

All: **Thanks be to God! Amen.**

Offering Prayer

One: We do not meet the persons our gifts reach;

All: **we cannot know their pain or enter their struggle.**

One: But with generous hearts, we give in faith, for we know that you,
   O God, will bless them.

All: **You will bless the compassion, the freedom, and the community these gifts make possible. Amen.**

Commissioning

One: You have seen the signs; you have heard the rumblings. Are you afraid?

All: **We have our Rock and we have our faith foundation; we will not fear!**

One: Jesus is your guide in the testing times; his life, his death, and his words are there when your world falls apart – a source of inspiration.

All: **We know where our trust belongs and, in the strength of our Christian community, we will win through! Thanks be to God!**

Proper 29 [34]

Reign of Christ or Christ the King Sunday

2 Samuel 23:1–7
Psalm 132:1–12, (13–18)
     or Daniel 7:9–10, 13–14 and Psalm 93
Revelation 1:4b–8
John 18:33–37

Call to Worship

One: In our circle of uncertainty and hurry,
All: you, O God, are the fixed point of calm.
One: In our stretched moments of stress and emotion,
All: you, O God, are the secure center of peace.
One: In our well-worn routine of the everyday,
All: you, O God, are the flash of fresh inspiration.
One: In our moments of the ordinary and the earthly,
**All: you, O God, are the Spirit that transforms and transcends
     with the Holy.**

Opening Prayer

One: Loving God, enable us to prepare for the reign of Christ.
**All: When the reign of Christ begins, all will be free to worship and to
     express their opinions.**
One: When the reign of Christ begins,
All: weapons of war will be destroyed and all children will be secure.
One: When the reign of Christ begins,
All: Mother Earth will be respected and her waters will be pure.
One: When the reign of Christ begins,
**All: prayer and praise will flow spontaneously to God and worship will
     be wholehearted and joyful.**
One: But when will the reign of Christ begin?
All: We will bring it closer! Amen.

A Prayer of Longing and Confession

One: We long for Christ's reign on earth; the poor and powerless will get a fair deal.

All: **Where we lack generosity, O God, encourage us to share.**

One: We long for Christ's reign on earth; the vulnerable ones will gain confidence.

All: **Where we lack confidence, O God, open our eyes to see the down-trodden.**

One: We long for Christ's reign on earth; those controlled and restricted will be free.

All: **Where we lack a liberating attitude, O God, enable us to work in new ways.**

One: We long for Christ's reign on earth; the faithful will be joyful and active in the community.

All: **Where we lack involvement, O God, open us to initiatives of compassion and participation.**

Time of reflection…

Words of Assurance

One: We will work to bring closer the reign of Christ.

All: **We will need new attitudes, renewed vision, and a change of heart.**

One: God will grant you the strength: spiritual, emotional, and practical.

All **We are ready!**

One: Pardon, peace, and a new determination are yours.

All: **Thanks be to God! Amen.**

Offering Prayer

One: "Your will be done on earth as it is in heaven…"

All: **We offer these gifts to you, O God, in the hope that the rule of Christ may increasingly be the rule for this nation and for this planet.**

One: Equip your church as the means by which the rule of Christ may be known:

All: **a rule of justice, a rule of compassion, a rule of acceptance, a rule of undying love.**

One: And equip each one of us to have a hand in establishing that rule, so that

All: **"Your will be done on earth as it is in heaven." Amen.**

Commissioning

One: Christ is our Ruler! We pledge our loyalty to him as we leave the church.

All: **We will acknowledge his loving leadership.**
We will follow his Way carefully.
We will serve others justly and carefully.
We will resist evil resolutely.
We will strive to establish his rule on earth.

Thanksgiving

2nd Monday in October (Canada), 4th Thursday in November (U.S.)

Joel 2:21–27
Psalm 126
1 Timothy 2:1-7
Matthew 6:25–33

Call to Worship

One: Show us the promise of spring, the flowering of summer, the glowing glory of fall,

All: **and our thanksgiving will be lasting, O God.**

One: Show us the smile on a baby's face, the fun of two children playing, an old person cracking a joke,

All: **and our thanksgiving will be joyful, O God.**

One: Show us one neighbor helping another, one family member sacrificing for another, the United Way going to work,

All: **and our thanksgiving will be thoughtful, O God.**

One: Show us the church caring for the vulnerable, worshipping whole-heartedly, learning enthusiastically,

All: **and our thanksgiving will be faithful, O God.**

Prayer of Thanksgiving

One: For a good meal after a long day, a star-filled sky, a hug from a loved one, an unexpected smile,

All: **thanksgiving flows naturally to you, O God.**

Choir: *Thanks for the things we need: food, clothes, warmth, and shelter.*

All: **Thanks for the people we love: parents and grandparents, friends near and far.**

Choir: *Thanks for a time to play: for soccer and baseball, crib and computer games.*

All: **Thanks for a time to dream: of faraway places, of luscious desserts, of family reunited, of freedom from worry.**

Choir: *Thanks for harvest gathered in and for useful work at the office, mill, and at home.*

All: **Thanks for our Christian faith: for prayer offered and answered, for the Good News Jesus brings, for joyful praise.**

One: Thanksgiving in all things:

Choir: when life is testing,

All: **in times of celebration,**

Choir: in times of sorrow.

All: **Thanksgiving to you, gracious God: faithful yesterday, faithful today, faithful all the days. Amen.**

Prayer of Reflection and Confession (based on Matthew 6:25–33)

One: We worry, God. We worry about work; we worry about family; we worry about our health. It seems so natural to worry.

All: **The words of Jesus challenge our anxieties: words that speak of your care, O God, for the smallest bird, for the most fragile flower.**

One: His words put our worries into perspective and secure us when our situation is unsettled, conflict-ridden, and shaking.

All: **The words of Jesus lift us from fear, reasoned and imagined, and save us from anger, bitter and consuming.**

One: His words call us to calm, to quiet, and to reflection. They are words to restore our confidence and our hope.

All: **The words of Jesus brought peace to the storm-tossed disciples and peace to the mentally sick.**

One: These words continue to still our anxieties for the faith community and its traditions, its readiness for mission, and its global vision.

All: **The words of Jesus embrace our fears for the world in which we are set, a world sorely in need of the Christian influence of peace.**

   Time of reflection…

Words of Assurance

One: In the quiet, you speak to us, O God; with resolve, you equip us; in faithfulness, you inspire us;

All: **and grant us your peace.**

One: Know the peace of God, which passes all understanding.

All: **God's new way stretches before us; God's forgiveness is reality for us. Thanks be to God! Amen.**

Offering Prayer

One: You will bless our offering, O God, if we dedicate our best gifts to you:

All: **our best talents to your service,**
our prime time to the Word and Way of Christ,
our commitment to those whom Christ would serve today.

One: Receive these gifts of money so that as they are used in the local and wider church, your name, O God, will be glorified.

Commissioning

One: Proclaim your thanksgiving! God is good! Rejoice in all God has given you.

All: **Declare God's greatness to those around you;**
work to build up the faith community;
share your blessings with the needy.

One: To love and understand God, look to Christ, your teacher and friend.

All Saints

November 1 or the first Sunday in November

Wisdom of Solomon 3:1–9 or Isaiah 25:6–9
Psalm 24
Revelation 21:1–6a
John 11:32–44

Call to Worship

One: Are you ready to worship God?

All: As those who have much to thank God for, we are ready!

One: Are you ready to follow Jesus?

All: As those who have heard his call to discipleship, we are ready!

One: Are you ready to work with the Spirit?

All: As those who are faithfully committed, we are ready!

One: Let us worship God!

Opening Prayer

One: Number us with the saints, O God;

All: give us a faithfulness that will not be shaken.

One: Number us with the saints, O God;

All: give us a will to serve that keeps on going.

One: Number us with the saints, O God;

All: give us a compassion that feels the deepest need.

One: Number us with the saints, O God;

All: give us a courage that will not compromise with the powerful ones.

One: Number us with the saints, O God;

All: give us the spirit of Jesus Christ to sustain us. Amen.

Prayer of Confession

(Use this model to include your own special saints!)

One: If Saint Paul was among us, he would ask,

All: "Are you prepared to radically change your ways in the light of new truth?"

One: If Saint Francis was among us, he would ask,

All: **"Are you prepared to live the simple life and serve the poor?"**

One: If Saint Thomas Becket was among us, he would ask,

All: **"Are you prepared to stand against the powerful ones, if it costs your livelihood or life itself?"**

One: If "Saint" Martin Luther King was among us, he would ask,

All: **"Are you prepared to risk humiliation and ridicule in order to bring freedom to the downtrodden?"**

> *Time of reflection...*

Words of Assurance

One: The role models we have often determine the way we act. Sometimes it is a family member, sometimes a good friend or neighbor, sometimes a saint from the history of the church, and sometimes a wise and holy one from a faith group very different from our own.

All: **We will search for those who show us the "most excellent way." We will take their way to heart and follow faithfully.**

One: And you will know the influence and the peace that Jesus showed so clearly.

All: **Thanks be to God! Amen.**

Offering Prayer

One: We could never offer enough to you, O God! You created us and it is through your goodness that we have come to this moment of time.

All: **We ask that you bless our gifts so that as they are used the work of your saints may be carried out in the just and compassionate way of Jesus Christ. Amen.**

Commissioning

One: The saints go with us from this church!

All: **Like Dietrich Bonhoeffer, may we hear God's call to faithful witness. Like Martin Luther King Jr., may we hear your call to justice. Like Mother Teresa, may we hear your call to compassion. Like Oscar Romero, may we hear your call to sacrifice.**

One: Send us forth, O God, in the saintly company, that we may be faithful to our high calling in Christ.

Memorial Day/Remembrance Day

Call To Worship

One: We remember those who fight against terror and fear-provokers

All: and we ask God's presence with them and with their families.

One: We remember those who in times past fought for freedom

All: and we are thankful for their sacrifice.

One: We remember those who lost homes and loved ones

All: and we are called to work for peace.

One: We remember those whose hearts are set on justice and reconciliation

All: and we will support and encourage them.

One: We remember that God's will is for all people to live in a harmonious and compassionate way.

All: We remember that the Way of Jesus is a way of peace.

Opening Prayer

One: Holy One, you have come close to us in Jesus Christ; you know the whole range of human experience. In times of joy and celebration, loving God,

All: you laugh with us; you strengthen us as family and as community.

One: In times of uncertainty and change, loving God,

All: you are the Rooted One; you hold us fast when the storm strikes home.

One: In times of loss, when our most cherished dreams have been snatched away from us, loving God,

All: you are the Enduring One, the voice of hope.

One: In times of warfare and terror, when it seems that calm will never return, loving God,

All: you are the Peaceful One, the promise of shalom.

Prayer of Affirmation (Confession)

One: This is the way we honor the memory of men and women ready to lay down their lives.

All: We will not tolerate hatred, nor stand idly by when innocent men, women, and children are killed and injured.

One: This is the way we honor those who help refugees and political prisoners.

All: **We will support them practically and challenge corrupt govern-ments to let the prisoners go free.**

One: This is the way we put an end to the conflict that is a part of our own experience.

All: **We will search out the source of our anger and sense what it means to walk in another's shoes.**

One: This is the way we will counter the influences of selfishness and fear, which are known to us.

All: **We will come humbly before you, O God, and take courage from the cross of Jesus the Christ.**

Time of reflection...

Words of Assurance

One: Let us look carefully at those ways in which our own lifestyle denies our Christian discipleship.

All: **We will take the time we need to come to fresh insights and understandings.**

One: Let us look carefully at our patterns of community life and service.

All: **We will take the time we need to plan a common life of faith.**

One: Pardon and peace are yours.

All: **Thanks be to God. Amen.**

Offering Prayer

One: Remember, your gifts are blessed by the Holy One!

All: **These gifts will promote a neighborhood where harmony and tolerance are the norm.**

These gifts will encourage a world where the developed nations share with those who have so little.

These gifts will bring the rejected and persecuted to a new land.

These gifts will be a means of healing and an end to fear.

These gifts will put the unsure on the road to confidence.

One: We offer them hopefully, O God.

All: **Amen.**

Commissioning

One: You leave this church with new thoughts and new intentions.

All: **We leave deeply grateful for all who gave their lives and for those scarred by war.**

We leave, as those realizing there is no short cut to peace.

We leave, as those committed to speak out against injustice.

We leave, as those prepared to model reconciliation.

We leave, as those ready to work to understand persons of different races and faiths.

One: You go hopefully and joyfully, for God, goes with you.

Thematic Index

Hebrew Scripture Index

New Testament Scripture Index